worshipping community

by
Joseph Lange, OSFS
and
Anthony J. Cushing

VOLUME II
OF THE
LIVING CHRISTIAN COMMUNITY
SERIES

ESS
Y./Paramus, N.J.

Acknowledgements

Scripture quotations, unless otherwise noted, were taken from *The New American Bible*, with the permission of the Confraternity of Christian Doctrine.

References marked TEV were taken from *Good News for Modern Man: The New Testament in Today's English Version*, copyrighted by The American Bible Society, 1966.

NIHIL OBSTAT
Msgr. James Mulligan
Censor Librorum

IMPRIMATUR
Most Rev. Joseph McShea, D.D.
Bishop of Allentown
October 31, 1975

Copyright © 1975 by
Paulist Fathers, Inc.
and Dove Publications

Library of Congress
Catalog Card Number: 75-34841

Published by
Paulist Press
Editorial Office: 1865 Broadway, N.Y., N.Y. 10023
Business Office: 400 Sette Drive, Paramus, N.J. 07652

ISBN: 0-8091-1919-6

and
Dove Publications
Pecos, New Mexico

Printed and bound in the
United States of America

Table of Contents

INTRODUCTION

Even a cursory study of the New Testament reveals the main elements of early Christian Church life. They are faith in the resurrected Jesus, the love of the Father, the power of the Holy Spirit, love for one another as expressed in communal life, hope in eternal life and in the Second Coming of Jesus, the breaking of the bread together (the Eucharist), and the presence of the Apostles.

The presence of the Apostles was important, essential really. They had spent three years with Jesus, learning from Him how to live by His word, His vision as Son of God. Their commission from Jesus is given in John 15, where Jesus says:

If you live in me,
and my words stay part of you,
you may ask what you will —
it will be done for you.
My Father has been glorified
in your bearing much fruit
and becoming my disciples.

(7-8)

It was not you who chose me,
it was I who chose you
to go forth and bear fruit.
Your fruit must endure,
so that all you ask the Father in my name
    he will give you.
The command I give you is this,
that you love one another.

(16-17)

When the Paraclete comes,
the Spirit of truth who comes from the Father
he will bear witness on my behalf.
You must bear witness as well,
for you have been with me from the beginning.

(26-27)

The Apostles had been with Jesus from the beginning of His public ministry. Their task was to carry on the mission of Jesus in the power of the Spirit: to proclaim to all men that God is calling together a new people, that He is making a New Covenant with all who would repent and accept Jesus as Savior and Lord, that all of us are called to be sons and daughters of the Father with Jesus, that all of us are called to share in His own Spirit, and that we are called to live together in love through the power of that same Holy Spirit.

The presence of the Apostles in the Church was later to be supplied by the word of God, the New Testament, their last will and testament to us.

In *Friendship with Jesus,* the first volume of this series, we have treated of repentance and faith in Jesus, of the Holy Spirit, and of hope in the Second Coming. In this volume, we want to treat the worshipping community, the new "people of God," the community of those whose love for one another is meant by Jesus to change the world. In subsequent volumes we will treat freedom and healing in Jesus, and the work of God's people, the Church.

All of these volumes deal with what is fundamental to the life of a follower of Jesus. There is no more or less important aspect of the Christian life, any more than one could say that one piece of a jigsaw puzzle is more or less important. It is not enough to love Jesus and be filled with His Spirit. In fact, I cannot say that I love Jesus unless I love His Body, my brothers and sisters in the Lord. In order to be fully transformed into Jesus, I must learn what it is to be part of God's people and how to live with others in a way that makes visible the new life together to which we are called in Christ.

This volume begins with teaching on the Lord's supper, both because it is a familiar community celebration for people of many denominations, and because it is the memorial which Jesus commands us to keep. In addition, in the prayers and actions of the liturgy, we find a summary of the core of our life together in Jesus.

The next three chapters treat of other aspects of the life of God's people, basic teachings of the Gospel. Some of it will take a bit of work to understand, but only if we make that effort will the Spirit be able to lead us more fully into the light. "A little hard work never hurt anybody," my mother used to say.

The last chapter in the volume deals with spiritual friendships. In an attempt to develop a community life we have been very conscious of the need to develop a life-style that everyone can follow. We have carefully avoided monastic community forms so that people from all walks of life can share in the community life. Intimate relationships are essential for growth, so we substitute spiritual friendships for households; and this chapter shares our experience with you.

May the Lord bless your efforts to draw close to Him by helping you to come closer to each other. How great His love is for us! How great His desire to make us His people!

May He be praised forever!

Joseph Lange, OSFS
Anthony J. Cushing

by Joseph Lange

The Lord's Supper 1

From the very beginning Christians gathered together to share in the Lord's supper. Acts describes the first Christian community, the Jerusalem community, this way: "They devoted themselves to the apostles' instruction and the communal life, to the breaking of bread and the prayers" (2:42).

Paul had to reprove the Corinthians and remind them of what he had taught them earlier about the Lord's supper:

What I now have to say is not said in praise, because your meetings are not profitable but harmful. First of all, I hear that when you gather for a meeting there are divisions among you, and I am inclined to believe it. There may even have to be factions among you for the tried and true to stand out clearly. When you assemble it is not to eat the Lord's Supper, for everyone is in haste to eat his own supper. One person goes hungry while another gets drunk. Do you not have homes where you can eat and drink? Would you show contempt for the church of God, and embarrass those who have nothing? What can I say to you? Shall I praise you? Certainly not in this matter!

I received from the Lord what I handed on to you, namely, that the Lord Jesus on the night in which he was betrayed took bread, and after he had given thanks, broke it and said, "This is my body, which is for you. Do this in remembrance of me." In the same way, after the supper, he took the cup, saying, "This cup is the new covenant in my blood. Do this, whenever you drink it, in remembrance of me." Every time, then, you eat this bread and drink this cup, you proclaim the death of the Lord until he comes! This means that whoever eats the bread or drinks the cup unworthily sins against the body and blood of the Lord. A man should examine himself first; only then should he eat

1

of the bread and drink of the cup. He who eats and drinks without recognizing the body eats and drinks a judgment on himself. That is why many among you are sick and infirm, and why so many are dying.

(I Cor. 11:17:30)

Later Christian writers called this supper "the Eucharist" (for example, the author of the *Didache,* a late first-century book, Ignatius of Antioch, and Justin). Later still it became known as "the Mass."

In the passages cited above several points stand out: (1) the early Christians were immediately led by the Spirit to a new form of communal life; (2) lack of unity is incompatible with sharing in the Lord's supper; (3) faith in the presence of the body and blood of Jesus is taught by Paul, who says he got it from the Lord (v. 23); (4) lack of faith or unity brings judgment on those who lack such faith or love; and (5) this judgment of the Lord shows itself among the Corinthians as sickness and death. It might also be noted that eating the Lord's supper was a daily occurrence among the Christians of the first Jerusalem community.

In later chapters we will treat of what it means to live in love, in the "unity of the Spirit." Here we want to discuss the sacred rite given us by the Lord to perpetuate until He comes, the rite which both symbolizes and brings about our life together in Jesus. To do this adequately, we must first look at the Jewish passover or *seder* or paschal meal; for it was at the paschal meal that Jesus gave us His memorial.

THE PASCHAL MEAL

The Paschal meal may have existed as a kind of spring festival prior to the exodus, but it soon afterwards became the celebration and memorial of the exodus (cf. Ex. 12:1-28). God had raised up Moses to lead the Hebrew people from slavery under the Egyptian Pharoah to the promised land. Since the Pharoah did not want to let his cheap labor escape, God sent a series of plagues upon Egypt to convince him that he could not resist God. The last of the plagues was announced to Pharoah by

2

Moses: in the middle of the night the firstborn son of every Egyptian would be slain, as well as the firstborn even of the animals. For their part the Israelites were to kill a spotless lamb and smear its blood on the doorposts of their houses so that God would "pass over" those homes and not kill their firstborn. They roasted the lamb whole and ate the meal standing with loins girt, staff in hand, ready for flight.

Following the passover and the death of all the firstborn in Egypt, the Israelites were driven from Egypt through the Red Sea, eventually arriving free in the promised land.

This is *the* saving event of Israel — God leading His people from slavery to freedom. Jews celebrate it yearly as the passover or paschal meal. Moreover, it is not just a celebration or anniversary. It is a "memorial," and a memorial is something special. A memorial is a ritual into which one enters as into an ongoing event. The redemptive action of God is recounted in the present tense. The participants become identified with the people of the original event. *We* are led out of slavery into freedom. God is *now* delivering us. We are all one people, regardless of distance and time. God's intervention is not something done only once in the past for our ancestors, but something done now for us, His people.

The paschal meal has changed during the centuries. It was once a sacrificial meal, with the lambs sacrificed in the temple at Jerusalem. When the temple was destroyed, there was no longer any place to offer sacrifice, so that element ceased.

Eating unleavened bread is part of the paschal meal because the Israelites had to leave so quickly that they did not have time to leaven their bread (the feast is sometimes called the Feast of Unleavened Bread for this reason). Jewish tradition requires that everything containing leaven be destroyed or removed from the house for the feast; for leaven, too, symbolizes evil. There is another symbolism here: eating unleavened bread means leaving evil behind and starting afresh.

The bitter herbs that are eaten remind everyone of the bitterness of slavery. A mixture of fruit, nuts, cinnamon and wine, reddish in color, brings to mind the mortar used by the Israelites in building the store-cities for the Egyptians.

3

Wine is drunk four times. The symbolism here is strong and deep. In the Bible men are often compared to grapes on the vine. But grapes must be crushed and fermented to become wine. The Israelites went through affliction to become free and to become united as a people. They drink the wine from a common vessel as a sign of unity.

All the food used in the paschal meal is blessed before it is eaten. The ritual begins with such a blessing, and the leader washes his hands to symbolize the cleansing necessary for all who share in the rite. The youngest present asks the question: "Why is this night different from all other nights? On all other nights we eat either leavened or unleavened bread. Why on this night do we eat only unleavened bread?" The answer is the narrative of the exodus.

Afterward there is a solemn prayer of thanksgiving (Greek: Eucharist). Next comes the supper in which the paschal lamb is eaten, followed by the breaking of a piece of unleavened bread and the drinking of the third and fourth cups of wine.

THE PASCHAL MEAL OF JESUS AND THE APOSTLES

All the Synoptic Gospels tell of this last passover meal that Jesus shared with His disciples (Matt. 26; Mark 14; Luke 22). Luke tells us that this is something which Jesus very much wanted to do: "I have greatly desired to eat the Passover with you before I suffer" (22:15). This was to be the last Jewish passover that they would share. Henceforth they would "memorialize" the New Covenant in the blood of the Lamb of God, Jesus Himself. Henceforth they would celebrate their new exodus from slavery in sin to freedom in Jesus.

During this last passover, Jesus changed the words of the blessings of the bread and wine. He tells us that this bread and wine will now be His body and blood of the New Covenant, and that we are to continue this memorial:

Then, taking bread and giving thanks, he broke it and gave it to them, saying: "This is my body to be given for you. Do this as a remembrance of me." He did the same with the cup after eating, saying as he did so: "This cup is the new covenant in my blood, which will be shed for you."

(Luke 22:19-20)

When Moses ratified the covenant at Sinai, he took the blood of young bulls, and after splashing half of it on the altar, he sprinkled the rest on the people, saying, "This is the blood of the covenant which the Lord has made with you in accordance with all these words of his" (Ex. 24:8).

Another point of some importance is the meaning of a covenant in Semitic culture. We remember that the American Indians used to close an agreement (covenant) with the ceremony of passing a "peace pipe." We do it by signing a paper, often affixing a seal. The Semitic people used to do it by having a meal together — and they took their covenants (agreements) seriously. It was their custom that a man who raised his hand against another with whom he had broken bread (shared a covenant meal) was to be stoned to death. So, another element of the Christian passover is the covenant meal. To share in it is to renew the covenant in Christ's blood: we are God's people and He is our God.

The symbolism of the Lord's supper is tremendously rich. As the Jews celebrate their deliverance from slavery and their becoming a people in covenant with God, so the Lord's supper celebrates the Christian passover, the deliverance from sin through the waters of baptism to freedom in Christ. Jesus becomes the sacrificial lamb, the innocent and spotless lamb slaughtered "for many," "for you," in whose blood the New Covenant is sealed. Communion with God and sharing in the saving event of Christ's passion, death, resurrection, and glorification take place by consuming the body and blood of Jesus present in the Eucharist. And, as Paul says in I Corinthians 10:17: "Because the loaf of bread is one, we, many though we are, are one body, for we all partake of the one loaf."

THE IMPLICATION FOR US

In a moment we shall look at the prayers of the Eucharist as we have it today and at the structure of the ritual. But, before we get to that, it is important to reflect on what we have already seen.

The Eucharist is meant to be the celebration of a people who know that they are a people and who know that they are God's people. Jesus gave us this "memorial" just for this purpose, to be celebrated "until He comes." This means quite obviously that unless we have this sense of being a people and of being God's people, then the Eucharist will not mean for us what it is supposed to mean. In fact, for most it will not mean anything at all.

On the other hand, it is certainly true that it is not enough for us to teach that this is what the Eucharist is *supposed* to be. If we examine our experience of anything else in life, we realize quite readily that it is *never* enough to teach what something is supposed to be. Nothing ever happens (or, at least, only rarely does anything happen) because we teach what is supposed to be.

Today we have so many people saying, "I don't get anything out of Mass," or "Mass doesn't mean anything to me." The answer is not just more words and more teaching, though these are essential. The answer is to begin to live *together,* as a people, as God's people. Only as we experience together God's love for us and our love for each other, only then will our gathering for the Eucharist take on significance as the coming together of God's people. The right kind of language and the right kind of experience together give us the sense that something is meaningful.

All kinds of efforts have been made and are being made to restore meaning to the Eucharist, and most of them are not at all helpful. We have to face the real problems if we are to come to real solutions, and the real problems are not being faced. The truth is that the Eucharist is not meaningful because: (1) people do not know Jesus personally, (2) the Spirit has not been released in their lives, and (3) there is no real community life in the Church. We have already dealt with (1) and (2) in the first volume of this series. In this and subsequent volumes we discuss various dimensions of community life in Jesus.

If we are to restore the Eucharist to the memorial that Jesus intends it to be, then we must begin to make some choices and do some new things. We must choose Him and His desire for our life together in His Spirit. We must choose to love the people He has called us to worship with. A really good start comes from every effort we can make to get to know each other. Another simple thing to do is to look around our church and our neighborhood and take an interest in those people who are close at hand. We will easily discover lonely and hurting people to whom we can bring a measure of comfort simply by offering our friendship. Where love is, God is. These are little things, simple things, but they can transform the life of our churches and our celebrations. In subsequent chapters and volumes we will develop all of this more fully.

It is also clear that we must talk to each other about what God is doing in our lives if we are to achieve a sense of being God's people. We cannot, we must not underestimate the damage that has been done because we have failed to let Jesus be the Lord of our conversations. We have not spoken of Him day in and day out as one with whom we are familiar; therefore we experience Him as far away. The world does not know how good our Father is because we do not share with each other how good He is. So many of the prayers of praise and thanksgiving for God's tender love and mighty works that we hear in the Lord's supper do not seem to apply to us, do not seem to mean anything to us simply because we do not tell each other what God is doing in our lives. Once we begin to share our lives with the Lord and share Him in our ordinary conversations, then these prayers will focus our own feelings and experiences of our good Father.

Another reason why the Eucharist does not accomplish what it is about (the celebration of the New Covenant) is our pre-Vatican II teaching and practice. As Catholics we have stressed the real presence of the glorified Lord in the Eucharist. We emphasized Benediction of the Blessed Sacrament and exposition and adoration. We fostered Forty Hours devotion and visits to Jesus in the tabernacle. Our churches were quiet places where we came to adore and say our prayers. For many, Mass was a time to say the rosary while the liturgy was read in Latin by the priest. We clearly felt that Mass was "said" by the priest and "witnessed" by the people.

Everything I have said so far shows how misplaced this emphasis was. It is true, certainly true, that Jesus is really present in the Eucharist; but the point is that He is present there in order to be the Lamb of God of the New Covenant which all of us share in. We have to make a shift in our perspective, which takes nothing away from Christ's real presence, but puts it into the context that He intends. Then we celebrate not only the first commandment, but the second as well. We gather as a people to celebrate the covenant in the blood of Jesus *as His people,* fully conscious of the brotherhood we share and of its consequences.

THE LORD'S SUPPER AS WE HAVE IT NOW

THE LITURGY OF THE WORD

In the Roman Church (and many other denominations) the Liturgy of the Eucharist is preceded by the Liturgy of the Word. It is a time of prayer, reading of the Scriptures, and reflections on these Scriptures. It is also one of the times we expect the Spirit to work among us to reveal His truth through the gifts of preaching and exhortation, teaching, words of knowledge and words of wisdom. As our churches become more and more open to the power of the Spirit, we can expect the charisms to be in evidence as we pray and reflect on God's words together.

One of the purposes of the liturgical reform has been to renew in Catholics the true place of God's word in their lives. For a number of reasons Catholicism has developed a sacramental piety over the past few centuries or more. Protestantism developed a biblical piety. In one case seeking God became primarily a matter of receiving sacraments and using popular devotions. In the other case, seeking God has been primarily a matter of being formed by God's word. Both have worked. Good Christians are to be found in all denominations. Today Catholics are being re-introduced to the Bible; other Christians are discovering the sacraments.

Because we Catholics have not been used to reading and studying the Bible, we need to work at it, to pay special attention to it. The liturgical reform since Vatican II is one element of this new effort. Each Sunday liturgy now presents three coordinated passages from the Bible, one from the Old Testament; one from the apostolic letters, Acts, or Revelation; and one from the Gospels. The readings are spread out over a three-year cycle so that the entire Bible will be proclaimed. Another change of considerable importance is the new direction that the sermon should be an explanation of the Scripture — a homily, and not just a talk on any old thing. In other words, the Liturgy of the Word is meant to be a weekly Bible study, in the context of the prayerful gathering of the people.

We all know that it is one thing to read or hear Scripture and quite another to be able to hear it in a way that touches us. For God's word to be God's-word-for-me, I have to be in a frame of mind that is receptive. Usually that means that I have to be *present* to His word, attentive, expecting it to make a difference, caring to hear what God wants to say to me. This is the reason for the structure, the liturgy, of the Word.

We begin with a hymn which should help us both to begin together to enter into the right frame of mind and, at the same time, introduce the theme of the readings for the day. Then the priest greets the people with "The Lord be with you" or some equivalent of that. This greeting really needs to be taken seriously. It is not just a "Hello!" but an invitation to remember that we are gathered in the Lord's presence. "The Lord be *with* you." He is here. Now. Be attentive to His presence.

As we focus our attention on His presence, we begin to experience all that we spoke about in *Friendship with Jesus* on the holiness of God and prayer. Prayer begins by entering the Sacred, the holy presence. There we feel, we know our insignificance, our sinfulness before God. So the ritual continues as the priest invites us to remember our sinfulness. This is certainly not meant to be a morbid preoccupation with our unworthiness, but rather the natural consequence of realizing into whose presence we have come. In addition, we are asked to confess our sinfulness or remember God's mercy, which means we are not asked to dwell on ourselves, but on God. True Christian repentance, like everything else Christian, is not self-centered. It is God and other-centered. Having acknowledged our sinfulness, we move on, we look up and rejoice in our God who is so very good.

The liturgy then naturally follows with a hymn of praise to God: "Glory to God in the highest." If we have not first entered into the Lord's presence, experienced our sinfulness, and turned our eyes in gratitude and wonder at our marvelous, forgiving Lord, then we have no reason to sing His praises. On the other hand, if we have entered into the movement of the liturgy so far, we want to praise God together.

> Glory to God in the highest,
>   and peace to his people on earth.
>
> Lord God, heavenly King,
> almighty God and Father,
>   we worship you, we give you thanks,
>   we praise you for your glory.
>
> Lord Jesus Christ, only Son of the Father,
> Lord God, Lamb of God.
> you take away the sin of the world:
>   have mercy on us;
> you are seated at the right hand of the Father:
>   receive our prayer.
>
> For you alone are the Holy one,
> you alone are the Lord,
> you alone are the Most High,
>   Jesus Christ,
>   with the Holy Spirit,
>   in the glory of God the Father.
>   Amen.

After we have entered into the Lord's presence, asked forgiveness for our sins and praised Him, the priest invites us to pray. In the period which follows, we may pray or sing in the Spirit, speaking to the Father our praise or thanksgiving or petition. Then the priest offers a prayer in the name of all.

Now we are ready to hear God's word. Now we are properly prepared. Still, we should *expect* God to speak to us in His word. Perhaps it will be only one word or one phrase from the readings or from the homily, but we should expect to be touched somehow. Our Father loves us very much. Why shouldn't He speak to our hearts when we gather for just that purpose? An expectant faith in hearing God's word is as important here as anywhere else.

The Liturgy of the Word ends with the recitation or singing of the Nicene Creed:

We believe in one God,
the Father, the Almighty,
maker of heaven and earth,
of all that is seen and unseen.

We believe in one Lord, Jesus Christ,
the only Son of God,
eternally begotten of the Father,
God from God, Light from Light,
true God from true God,
begotten, not made, one in Being with the Father.
Through him all things were made.
For us men and for our salvation
he came down from heaven:
by the power of the Holy Spirit
he was born of the Virgin Mary, and became man.

For our sake he was crucified under Pontius Pilate;
he suffered, died, and was buried.
On the third day he rose again
in fulfillment of the Scriptures;
he ascended into heaven
and is seated at the right hand of the Father.
He will come again in glory
to judge the living and the dead,
and his kingdom will have no end.

We believe in the Holy Spirit, the Lord, the giver of life,
who proceeds from the Father and the Son.
With the Father and the Son
he is worshipped and glorified.
He has spoken through the Prophets.
We believe in one holy catholic and apostolic Church.
We acknowledge one baptism for the forgiveness of sins.
We look for the resurrection of the dead,
and the life of the world to come.

Amen.

In the early centuries the Liturgy of the Word was the time of instruction for prospective converts to Christianity. The instruction period usually lasted from one to two years! Baptism took place during the Easter vigil service. That service is still celebrated in the Roman Church.

After the Liturgy of the Word was completed, those under instructions who were not yet baptized into Jesus and His Spirit were asked to leave. The eucharistic celebration was for those who were members of Christ's Body, filled with His Spirit.

THE LITURGY OF THE EUCHARIST

As with the ancient passover ritual, the Eucharist begins with the blessing of the food. Each blessing expresses God's goodness, the goodness of His earth, and the goodness of the human work which produces the bread and the wine. We sometimes forget the goodness of God's world or of our own work. We sometimes encounter those who have condemned God's creation or who have so minimized man's part in salvation that man's efforts appear useless or even evil. These prayers remind us that truths do not stand in opposition to each other, but in a beautiful harmony. God's blessings come to us through the world that He has so wonderfully created, as we work with what He has given us.

It is true that God gives us everything. It is true that the world (nature) works in a certain way. It is true that man's work is both good and necessary. All three are true at once.

The prayers end with an expression of faith that the bread and wine will become for us the "bread of life" and "our spiritual drink."

Before the blessing of the wine, a little water is mixed with it to symbolize our union with Jesus in His blood. The accompanying prayer reminds us that we share in the divinity of Christ, i.e., we share in the same Holy Spirit which makes us one Body with Christ.

> Blessed are you, Lord, God of all creation. Through your goodness we have this bread to offer, which earth has given and human hands have made. It will become for us the bread of life.

> By the mystery of this water and wine may we come to share in the divinity of Christ, who humbled himself to share in our humanity.

> Blessed are you, Lord, God of all creation. Through your goodness we have this wine to offer, fruit of the vine and work of human hands, it will become our spiritual drink.

THE EUCHARISTIC PRAYER

After a ritual washing of hands to symbolize our need for purification before entering the presence of God, the Eucharistic Prayer begins with an invitation to praise God. (Praise is always the appropriate way to begin prayer.)

> P. The Lord be with you.
> R. And also with you.
> P. Lift up your hearts.
> R. We lift them up to the Lord.
> P. Let us give thanks to the Lord our God.
> R. It is right to give him thanks and praise.

Then follows the hymn of praise called the "Preface." There are dozens of them in the new ritual. An example:

13

Father, all powerful and ever-living God,
We do well always and everywhere to give you thanks
through Jesus Christ our Lord.
Through Christ you bring to us
    the knowledge of your truth,
that we may be united by one faith and one baptism
    to become his body.
Through Christ you have given
    the Holy Spirit to all peoples.
How wonderful are the works of the Spirit,
    revealed in so many gifts!
Yet how marvelous is the unity
    the Spirit creates from their diversity,
as he dwells in the hearts of your children,
    filling the whole church with his presence,
    and guiding it with his wisdom.
In our joy, we sing to your glory
    with all the choirs of angels.

Then the people respond with the beautiful words of the Seraphim from Isaiah 6 and the words of the people at Christ's triumphal entry into Jerusalem:

Holy, Holy, Holy Lord, God of power and might,
    heaven and earth are filled with your glory.
Hosanna in the highest.
Blessed is he who comes in the name of the Lord.
Hosanna in the highest.

Each of the four Eucharistic Prayers contains the following elements:

1. Praise of the Father. The whole of the liturgy is directed to the Father through the Son in the power of the Spirit.

2. Invocation of the Holy Spirit. That the bread and wine may become the body and blood of Jesus, the resurrected Christ, we call on the power of the Spirit.

3. A narrative of the Lord's supper. The setting is the passover meal. Jesus departs from the usual ritual. After the thanksgiving and praise, He gives the bread and the wine to His disciples as His body and His blood, given for us (as sacrifice), the meal of the New Covenant.

4. A memorial acclamation. Following the narrative, the people proclaim what God has done in Jesus.

5. Offering. The Church, particularly the Church assembled right there and then, offers this one acceptable sacrifice to the Father for the salvation of all of us.

6. A second invocation of the Holy Spirit. This time we are reminded why we are given the Spirit as we pray to be filled anew: *so that* we might become one. We are at the Lord's supper as God's people (the Church) made so by the Holy Spirit, called to unity *and* empowered by the Spirit for that unity.

7. Intercession. These are prayers of the Church for the whole Church living and dead in communion with all those in Christ from the beginning. We are all one Body, one communion of the saints.

8. Finally, a prayer of praise confirmed by a great Amen.

An example of the Eucharistic Prayer (No. 3) is included below for your meditation. Pray it. Ponder it. Take it line by line. Make notes on what the Lord says to you through it.

Praise of the Father
> Father, you are holy indeed,
> and all creation rightly gives you praise.
> All life, all holiness comes from you
> through your Son, Jesus Christ our Lord,
> by the working of the Holy Spirit.
> From age to age you gather a people to yourself,
> so that from east to west
> a perfect offering may be made
> to the glory of your name.

Invocation of the Holy Spirit
> And so, Father, we bring you these gifts.

15

We ask you to make them holy
   by the power of your Spirit,
that they may become the body and blood
of your Son, our Lord Jesus Christ,
at whose command we celebrate this eucharist.

The Narrative

On the night he was betrayed,
he took bread and gave you thanks and praise.
He broke the bread, gave it to his disciples, and said:
Take this, all of you, and eat it:
this is my body which will be given up for you.

When supper was ended, he took the cup.
Again he gave you thanks and praise,
gave the cup to his disciples, and said:
Take this, all of you, and drink from it:
this is the cup of my blood,
the blood of the new and everlasting covenant.
It will be shed for you and for all men
so that sins may be forgiven.
Do this in memory of me.

Memorial Acclamation

Christ has died,
Christ is risen,
Christ will come again!

Offering

Father, calling to mind the death your son endured
   for our salvation.
his glorious resurrection and
   ascension into heaven,
and ready to greet him when he comes again,
we offer you in thanksgiving
   this holy and living sacrifice.

Look with favor on your Church's offering,

and see the Victim whose death
    has reconciled us to yourself.

Second Invocation of the Spirit

Grant that we, who are nourished
    by his body and blood,
may be filled with his Holy Spirit,
and become one body, one spirit in Christ.

Intercessions

May he make us an everlasting gift to you
and enable us to share
    in the inheritance of your saints,
with Mary, the virgin Mother of God;
with the apostles, the martyrs,
and all your saints,
on whose constant intercession
    we rely for help.

Lord, may this sacrifice,
which has made our peace with you,
advance the peace and salvation
    of all the world.
Strengthen in faith and love
    your pilgrim Church on earth;
your servant, Pope Paul, our bishop,
and all the bishops,
with the clergy and the entire people
    your Son has gained for you.
Father, hear the prayers of the family
    you have gathered here before you.
In mercy and love unite all your children
    wherever they may be.

Welcome into your kingdom our departed
    brothers and sisters,
and all who have left this world in your friendship.
We hope to enjoy for ever the vision of your glory,

through Christ our Lord,
from whom all good things come.

Concluding Praise

Through him,
with him,
in him,
in the unity of the Holy Spirit,
all glory and honor is yours,
almighty Father,
for ever and ever.

Amen!

THE COMMUNION RITE

We begin the Communion rite by praying together the
Lord's prayer. The priest then expands the last petition:

Deliver us, Lord, from every evil,
and grant us peace in our day.
In your mercy keep us free from sin
and protect us from all anxiety
as we wait in joyful hope
for the coming of our Savior, Jesus Christ.

And the people reply with an ancient conclusion:

For the kingdom, the power, and the glory are yours,
now and forever.

Next is a rite of peace. Before we approach God's altar, He
asks us to be at peace with one another. The priest says a prayer
reminding Jesus of His gift of peace to us, asking Him to grant
us that gift. Then the priest invites everyone to share some sign
of peace. This is ritual, a symbolic gesture whose significance
goes far beyond its immediate action. Shaking hands with or
embracing one or two others symbolizes my peace with all men.
My taking this gesture of peace seriously and meaning it prepares
my heart for the sharing in Communion.

The priest then breaks the bread, symbolic of the "breaking
of the bread" at the last supper, and the people say or sing:

Lamb of God, you take away the sins of the world,
have mercy on us.
Lamb of God, you take away the sins of the world,
have mercy on us.
Lamb of God, you take away the sins of the world,
grant us peace.

Jesus is the Lamb of God, slaughtered like an animal for the forgiveness of sins, the passover or paschal lamb of the New Covenant.

The priest then quietly offers a prayer in preparation for his own Communion. I think it is significant that in each of the two optional prayers in the ritual there is a prayer for healing:

By your holy body and blood
free me from all my sins and from every evil.

Let it not bring me condemnation,
but health in mind and body.

Encountering Jesus in the Eucharist is encountering the healing, forgiving Lord. We should expect Him to forgive and heal us.

The priest then holds up a particle of the consecrated bread, and says:

This is the Lamb of God
who takes away the sins of the world.
Happy are those who are called to his supper.

The people respond by expressing their faith in the healing power of Jesus:

Lord, I am not worthy to receive you,
but only say the word and I shall be healed.

After Communion there is a period of silence or song. It can also be a time for an inspired exultation, if the Lord gives such a word to someone in the community.

Then the priest prays for God's blessings for everyone and sends them on their way:

Go in peace to love and serve the Lord.

The ritual ends with a hymn.

When you celebrate the Eucharist together, remember us. We remember you.

BIBLIOGRAPHY

RECOMMENDED READING:

The prayers of the Roman Mass. (See a missal or a parish missalette.)
It is well worth the time to meditate on the prayers of the Mass.

Grailville, *The Paschal Meal,* Abbey Press, St. Meinrad, Indiana, 1973, 31pp.
Besides a short introduction relating to the Mass and the Passover meal, this booklet contains an arrangement of the last supper as a ceremony which can be carried out by a family, prayer group, etc.

Evely, Louis, *Credo,* Fides Publishers, Inc., Notre Dame, Indiana, 1967, 179pp.
Evely examines the Apostles' Creed and the Nicene Creed article by article. Full of insights. Really valuable.

by Joseph Lange

The Church: Body of Christ 2

If we take the time to study the Scriptures, we discover that Jesus did, in fact, come to bring "peace on earth to men of good will." The peace which He gives is for now, to men of good will *on earth*. His whole way of life and all of His teaching are God's gift to us to help us here and now, as human beings, achieve the peace which He gives.

He began His ministry by preaching repentance. He said that if we are to find peace in ourselves and peace with each other, we must begin with ourselves. We must acknowledge our sinfulness before God and before each other. We must ask forgiveness. We must get into a right relationship with God and with our neighbor. He tells us that the peace He offers comes from living in love and forgiveness with Him and with all men.

He shared His life with twelve men for three years. These were to be His Apostles. This training consisted in: (1) being with Him, (2) hearing His teaching, (3) witnessing His power, (4) sharing a life together day in and day out, and (5) witnessing His death and resurrection. Then, having received His Spirit, they were sent out to serve.

He taught them about the Father's love, how to get along with each other, how to pray. He intervened in their quarrels. He answered their questions. He gave an example to them.

He formed them into a people, the "remnant" spoken of in so many of the Old Testament prophecies. Many years later, Peter, recalling Exodus 19:6, spoke of us as "a chosen race, a royal priesthood, a holy nation, a people He claims for His own..." (I Pet. 2:9). Jesus came to form a people, a holy people, God's people, the people of the New Covenant. This is

21

what the word "Church" means: *ek-klesia,* "a-people-called-out," or "the assembly of those called."

Jesus came to form a people. He started with twelve, and to one of them, Peter, He said: "I for my part declare to you, you are 'Rock,' and on this rock I will build my church, and the jaws of death shall not prevail against it" (Matt. 16:18). The mission of the Apostles would be to form a people, the people of the New Covenant in the blood of Jesus. Living together as a people with their God, they would find that peace which Jesus gives.

Jesus came to form a people. This is what the prophets of old had foretold:

> The days are coming, says the Lord, when I will make a new covenant with the house of Israel and the house of Judah. It will not be like the covenant I made with their fathers the day I took them by the hand to lead them forth from the land of Egypt; for they broke my covenant, and I had to show myself their master, says the Lord. But this is the covenant which I will make with the house of Israel after those days, says the Lord. I will place my law within them, and write it upon their hearts; I will be their God, and they shall be my people.
>
> (Jer. 31:31-33)

> I will sprinkle clean water upon you to cleanse you from all your impurities, and from all your idols I will cleanse you. I will give you a new heart and place a new spirit within you, taking from your bodies your stony hearts and giving you natural hearts . . . you shall be my people, and I will be your God.
>
> (Ex. 36:25-28)

Nowhere does God in His word speak *only* of a personal choice for Jesus. Through His word He formed a people for Himself, the people of the Old Covenant. Through His Word-Made-Flesh He forms a new people of the New Covenant. We now are His people; He is our God.

The general theological perspective of *Friendship with Jesus* brought out the contrast between living in the world and living in the family of God. Our chapter on "The Lord's Supper" reminds us of the way Jesus wants us to celebrate our covenant until He comes: it is the celebration of a people who know they are a people and who act that way. In subsequent chapters and in the next two volumes we want to work out in more detail what it means to be God's people. The point we wish to make in this chapter is simple: we are called together to be a people. We will look at the teaching of Jesus and the Apostles, the example of Christians through the ages, and some contemporary problems.

THE TEACHING OF JESUS

Throughout the Gospels we find Jesus calling us to trust and love our God; to trust, love, and forgive our neighbor. In the Sermon on the Mount, Matthew puts together many sayings of Jesus which point out differences between the Old and New Covenants. Now we are called upon to restrain our temper, to purify our hearts, to offer no resistance to injury, to love our enemies, to avoid hypocrisy, to shun all judgments, to trust totally in our Father in heaven. Jesus relentlessly exposes the truth of what it is to be human and what it is to be real. He cuts through our games and our phoniness and shows us that we can never live together in love until we come to grips with the truth, until we are delivered from the shackles of possessiveness and greed and lust and self-centeredness. He teaches us and shows us to forgive from our hearts, so that we might be united.

THE KINGDOM

The whole mission of Jesus was to found the new Kingdom of God, a people who would live together in love under the reign of God. All His teaching is directed towards this goal. Every· bit of advice He gives to us as individuals is so that we can come together as a people in whom God's presence and love and power are visible in our life together.

Our life together is the life of a Messianic people. The reign of God has broken in. The life and love and power of God are to be manifest in the life of His people. All the signs of the Spirit in the person of Jesus are signs of the reign (Kingdom) of

23

God in the New Covenant. In Matthew 10 we read of Jesus
calling the twelve together and sending them out:

> Then He summoned His twelve disciples and gave them
> authority to expel unclean spirits and to cure sickness and
> disease of every kind.
>
> (1)
>
> As you go, make this announcement: 'The reign of God is
> at hand!' Cure the sick, raise the dead, heal the leprous,
> expel demons. The gift you have received, give as a gift.
>
> (7-8)

This little band of twelve is the mustard seed, the leaven, the
salt of the earth, the remnant of the old which will be the seed
of the new.

PEACE AND DIVISION

Jesus also tells them something which seems to contradict
His offer of peace:

> Do not suppose that my mission on earth is to spread
> peace. My mission is to spread, not peace, but division. I
> have come to set a man at odds with his father, a daughter
> with her mother, a daughter-in-law with her mother-in-law:
> in short, to make a man's enemies those of his own
> household. Whoever loves father or mother, son or
> daughter, more than me is not worthy of me. He who will
> not take up his cross and come after me is not worthy of
> me. He who seeks only himself brings himself to ruin,
> whereas he who brings himself to naught for me discovers
> who he is.
>
> (Matt. 10:34-39)

Jesus does bring peace. But the peace He offers costs
something. Jesus offers the truth, the truth about ourselves,
about the world, about life. That truth is a two-edged sword. It
can bring division because once it is revealed, it calls for a
decision. "He who is not with me is against me," Jesus says.
There is no middle ground here. Jesus is the Truth. We are
called upon to accept or reject. In a family, among friends, some
will accept, some will reject. Either Jesus is chosen as Savior and

24

Lord or He is offensive. Either we see Him as the answer to our weakness and sinfulness, or we are offended by His very presence, His very name. Men do not like to be reminded of their weaknesses, their flaws. The presence of Jesus is a light which reveals those flaws and weaknesses. Anger, resentment, and flight are common responses to Jesus. So, Jesus is peace and life to those who accept Him; but since not all do accept Him, divisions will occur.

MOLDING A PEOPLE

Jesus came to form a people. Nowhere is this more apparent than in the way He chose to spend the years of His ministry. He did not wander about alone. He selected twelve men to share life with. They walked together, ate together, slept together, lived together. They had a common treasury. They shared their weaknesses and their strengths. In one place He said, "Where two or three are gathered in my name, there am I in their midst" (Matt. 18:20). The important phrase is "gathered in my name." That does not mean being in the same place and using the name of Jesus. Nor does it mean simply being together for some Christian purpose. It means being Jesus for each other. The Hebrew notion of doing something "in the name of another" is to do it as he would. To be gathered in the name of Jesus is to be Jesus for each other. To be loving, forgiving, merciful, and Spirit-filled. Then He is there in us and between us.

At the appointed time, after three years of intimate life together, Jesus gathered with His Apostles for the last supper. In John's Gospel we find His last talk with them. In chapter 15 we read:

This is my commandment:
love one another
as I have loved you.
There is no greater love than this:
to lay down one's life for one's friends.
You are my friends
if you do what I command you.
I no longer speak of you as slaves,
for a slave does not know

what his master is about.
Instead, I call you friends,
since I have made known to you
all that I heard from my Father.

(12-15)

Jesus' command to us is to love as He has loved us. That is
what He is all about. Then we will be a people, His people —
and more, no longer slaves, but friends.

We are to live together in His name. That means that we live
in deep, real love for each other, seeking together to do the
Father's will. The tower of Babel keeps coming to my mind. A
lot of men got together to build it. It was their project, not
God's. It ended up in confusion. In the end no one could
understand the other. They spoke different languages.

We all come from different backgrounds with different
interests and different abilities. As a people, the only thing we
have in common is Jesus. The only task we have together is the
will of the Father. On these grounds we can be of one mind and
one heart. With these roots we can be one people.

In our own community we have often enough had our own
towers of Babel. Some projects have ended in confusion and the
breakdown of communication because what we were doing was
not His will or because we were not seeking it. We have learned
that the most important question in the discussion of any
project is: what does the Lord want?

"This is my commandment: love one another as I have loved
you." As we do that, we become a people, His people.

A little later, in chapter 17 of John, Jesus says something
even more powerful:

I pray also for those who will believe in me
    through their word,
that all may be one
as you, Father, are in me, and I in you;
I pray that they may be [one] in us,
that the world may believe that you sent me.
I have given them the glory you gave me
that they may be one, as we are one —
I living in them, you living in me —

that their unity may be complete.
So shall the world know that you sent me,
and that you loved them as you loved me.

(20-23)

ONENESS

Read that passage again.

Then, read it again and again and again and again. Read it every day of your life, and still you will not be able to comprehend it! Jesus prays that we may be as close to each other as He is to the Father! Can you understand that? What kind of people must we be to be that close to each other? Jesus prays that our unity may be complete! Can you imagine that? Have you anywhere, anytime experienced such a unity among human beings?

And, yet, Jesus prays for this unity among us "that the world may believe that you sent me." This unity, this "gathered in His name," is to be the sign of the authenticity of Jesus' mission. Perhaps it is no wonder that the world does not believe. Where does one find Christians who are so united? In what way have you contributed to the life of unity with the Christians of your own church? Do you have a passionate desire to bring peace and unity?

Do you begin to get the idea that we are very far from being what Jesus wants us to be together? Do you begin to see that it is not enough to choose Jesus as Savior and Lord and be baptized in the Spirit? Do you begin to see that Jesus came to bring us together? Do you begin to sense the futility of such a vision?

I look around the church where I worship and I do not even know most of the people there, let alone love them. Can we *really* become one as Jesus and the Father are one? I look around my neighborhood and I find that I do not know my neighbors. I do not really know the people I work with. We are not a people as God wants us to be a people, and what with all of our own worries and fears and selfishness, how can we ever become one?

Jesus knew this. He knew our helplessness, our weakness,

27

our self-centeredness. He knew how much we want our own way and how destructive that is. So at the same time that He tells us His commandment to love one another as He loves us, He promises us the Holy Spirit, the Helper (Greek: Paraclete), so that we can know and love as He does. In subsequent chapters and volumes we work this out more fully. We cannot say everything at once. Here we only want to point up the call to unity and its solution in the Holy Spirit. Jesus both commands and empowers us to love. Praise God!

THE JERUSALEM COMMUNITY

On the first Pentecost, Peter, filled with the Holy Spirit, boldly preached repentance. He called the people to faith in Jesus. Some responded that day, others followed as the preaching continued. The first work of the Spirit is to give faith. The second is to bring people together in Jesus. Luke describes the first converts this way:

> They devoted themselves to the apostles' instruction and the communal life, to the breaking of bread and the prayers. A reverent fear overtook them all, for many wonders and signs were performed by the apostles. Those who believed shared all things in common; they would sell their property and goods, dividing everything on the basis of each one's need. They went to the temple area together every day, while in their homes they broke bread. With exultant and sincere hearts they took their meals in common, praising God and winning the approval of all the people.
>
> (Acts 2:42-47; cf. also 4:32ff)

The important words here are "in common" and "together." That the particular way in which they worked out their life together was a matter of selling property and goods is not important. There are other ways. What is important is that we see how the work of the Spirit is love, coming together, a life in common. All the other works of the Spirit are to this end, for the Spirit completes the work of Jesus.

The immediate response of the first believers in Jesus was to form a common life in which everyone was cared for, a life of love and common worship. It has been so ever since. Every new outpouring of the Spirit through the centuries either grew out of common life or led to it.

Does this frighten you? Do you think, perhaps, that this is for someone else, but not you? If you have heard the call of Jesus to receive His Spirit, and if you understand what it means to be part of His people, then I can understand that it would be frightening. The call of Jesus is revolutionary. He calls us to a whole new family, a new way of life with each other, a leaving behind of the old and a putting on of the new.

For some, answering the call of Jesus is frightening; for some, receiving the gifts of the Spirit is frightening. It is something new and unknown, and it means stepping out in faith. If your faith has expanded to include the Spirit and His gifts, now realize that your faith must be expanded yet another step to include the common life with other believers until we become of one mind and one heart. This is not a matter for discussion, but for decision, a decision of faith. It will take the rest of this series to work out the dimensions of it.

THE TEACHING OF PAUL

There is no need to review all the epistles of all the Apostles to show how the message of love is found there. Read them. See how their years with Jesus and their life of sharing in the Christian communities is expressed so clearly in their concerns. Paul, however, is worth looking at specifically because of the way he develops the theology of the Body of Christ.

Everywhere he went Paul formed Christian communities: churches. Sooner or later all of them had problems with teaching or morals or discipline, and Paul wrote to some of them to deal with the problems. In Corinth a host of difficulties had arisen, such as factionalism, incest, lawsuits before pagans, etc. When they gathered for worship and the Lord's supper, there were all sorts of disorders; and even the use of the spiritual gifts was a cause of controversy. Paul responded by placing the areas of conflict in the larger context of why the believers were called together in Christ.

THE BODY OF CHRIST

In chapter 12, after speaking of the gifts of the Spirit, Paul moves on to a discussion of the Body of Christ. He points out that every part of the Body is important, that though there are differences we are all one Body. So, there must be no dissension, no division. "If one members suffers, all the members suffer with it; if one member is honored, all the members share its joy" (I Cor. 12:26).

We are members of one another. We are one Body and that is the Body of Christ (13 and 27). In chapter 10 Paul links the Body of Christ to the Eucharist:

Is not the cup of blessing we bless a sharing in the blood of Christ? And is not the bread we break a sharing in the body of Christ? Because the loaf of bread is one, we, many though we are, are one body, for we all partake of one loaf.

(16, 17)

Another way of speaking about our new unity in one Body is to speak of the Messianic Presence or of the "Word-Made-Flesh." The fullness of the Spirit-in-the-flesh was found in Jesus, Emmanuel, God-with-us. The New Covenant, the age of the Spirit, was all contained and manifested in Jesus. In Him we find the characteristics of the work of the Spirit: the presence of God and the power of God shown in the forgiveness of sins, miracles, healings, prophecy, anointed teaching, etc. In Jesus the Spirit was limited to the space and time of Jesus' own presence. However, Jesus passed on His Spirit to us so that in us together the Messianic Presence might continue and spread over all the earth. We are the Body of Christ, and in us together are to be found all the manifestations of the Spirit found in Jesus. Anyone encountering a local church, the local Body of Christ, should find in the assembly all the works of Jesus: the healing, forgiving, merciful love, the healings and miracles, etc. We are the Body of Christ. Our life together is meant to be the Messianic Presence to the world.

The solution to the problems of Corinth, Paul points out, is to remember who we are, what our life together is. There must be order. There must be peace. There must be love and unity. The Spirit manifests Himself through gifts and ministries, but these must be exercised in a love and humility which allows the unity of the Body to grow and find expression.

We are no longer our own. We have been baptized into the one Body of Christ, filled with the Spirit of God. Separation, isolation, withdrawal are illusions, even betrayals of the Good News. A life-style which is not community oriented is an obstacle to the reign of God. It is self-centered and ugly. Life in the Spirit is a life together in the power of God.

Paul says the same thing to the Romans: "Just as each of us has one body with many members, and not all the members have the same function, so too we, though many, are one body in Christ and individually members one of another" (12:4-5).

And to the Ephesians:

> I plead with you, then, as a prisoner for the Lord, to live a life worthy of the calling you have received, with perfect humility, meekness, and patience, bearing with one another lovingly. Make every effort to preserve the unity which has the Spirit as its origin and peace as its binding force. There is but one body and one Spirit, just as there is one hope given all of you by your call. There is one Lord, one faith, one baptism; one God and Father of all, who is over all, and works through all, and is in all.
>
> (4:1-6)

We are the Body of Christ. He is the Head. We are filled with the same Spirit. Being baptized into Jesus, the Father sees us as part of Jesus. Because of that, because we are Christ's Body, we share in all that He is. We share in His priesthood, in His power, in His mission. And, because the Spirit of God transcends all time, we are members of one another with all who ever have been or ever will be baptized into the one Body.

IN CHRIST

Together we are the Body of Christ ever present to the Father as the sacrificial lamb. We are part of the one acceptable sacrifice of Jesus on the cross. We are nailed to the cross with

Christ. We make up in our bodies what is lacking in the suffering of Christ. We are the extensions of His Body in time and place. We have died with Him and risen with Him to a new life of glory. We do not need to be great pray-ers. We are in Christ and He is in us. We are not made holy by our works. Rather, He works in us. He prays in us. All things are through, with, and in Christ to the glory of the Father. Amen.

This is what the New Covenant is about. This is what the Age of the Spirit is about. We are the Messianic Presence which is to be a mustard seed, a leaven which will spread through the whole world and bring all creation together in Christ.

Think of it! Think of the power of it! Think of the privilege of it! As we open our hearts in faith, as we come together making every effort to become united in the Spirit, as we allow the Spirit to work in power through us together, the world will know that Jesus is alive and that He loves us.

Every parish and church must come again to the vision of what it is called to be, the Body of Christ, joined in love and service to every other local manifestation of Christ's Body. Every church, conscious of its mission, must become a Messianic Presence, filled with the healing, forgiving love of Jesus, manifesting the power of the Spirit in the sense of God's presence and in healings and miracles and prophecy, etc.

It should be pointed out, too, that for Paul the Church as the Body of Christ is not just a metaphor, not just a figure of speech. It is entirely original with Paul, and for him it is real. Our bodies are part of the Body of Christ. In I Corinthians 6 Paul deals with the problems of sexual immorality by reminding us that our bodies are members of Christ's Body:

> Do you not see that your bodies are members of Christ? Would you have me take Christ's members and make them the members of a prostitute? God forbid! Can you not see that the man who is joined to a prostitute becomes one body with her? Scripture says, "The two shall become one flesh." But whoever is joined to the Lord becomes one spirit with him.

(15-17)

We are the Body of Christ. Where we are, Christ is. Together

32

we are the Messianic Presence. Praise God!

THE WITNESS OF HISTORY

Throughout the centuries, from apostolic times until today, the presence and power of God showing through His people have drawn men to Jesus. Acts describes some of what went on in apostolic times: the formation of churches, the development of ministries and leadership, the miracles and healings and gifts of the Spirit. The Good News was preached in the power of the Spirit with signs and wonders. Christianity spread throughout the world.

This Messianic Presence continued for centuries. St. Augustine's church in Hippo was the scene of many healings, even of people being raised from the dead. After the barbarian invasions Europe was re-Christianized with the same outpouring of the Spirit and the same manifestations. The Franciscan renewal of the thirteenth century was the same. The founding of religious communities was always accompanied by signs and wonders, too.

In a series of articles in *New Covenant* magazine, Ed Ensley describes the charismatic life in the Church from a variety of sources. This is not only what the Church is supposed to be. It is what the Church has been. The Lord is seeing to it that it will be so again!

Many of the renewal movements through the centuries began as charismatic outpourings. The life of the people so touched has resembled in many ways the current charismatic renewal. Unfortunately, many of the renewal movements of the past resulted in schism, in breaking away, in separation rather than unity.

PENTECOSTALISM

In the twentieth century we have seen a new outpouring of the Spirit in the form of Pentecostalism. An outgrowth of the Holiness movement of the eighteenth and nineteenth centuries, manifestations of the Spirit were not new in Pentecostalism. The camp meetings in the nineteenth century were full of healings and miracles and tongues, and people flocked to these meetings where God's power and presence could be experienced.

In the early 1900's, primarily from Azusa Street in Los Angeles (though similar revivals were occurring simultaneously in other parts of the world), Pentecostalism began to spread throughout the United States and the world. The historic churches reacted against it, and the newly Spirit-filled people left their churches to form new ones. Those later split into at least twenty-five separate denominations and a couple of hundred sects. New churches began to be founded everywhere, and Pentecostalism has long since been recognized as the third force in Christianity alongside Catholicism and Protestantism. Today Pentecostalism is by far the fastest growing of the three.

In Pentecostalism we encounter an expectant faith through which God's Spirit can work; therefore its prayer groups and assemblies are filled with God's presence and power. The preaching is anointed and accompanied by signs and wonders. Converts are made and the church grows.

The story is not all good, though. The continued divisions and factions point, not to the work of the Spirit, but to the flesh. And, further, as was inevitable, once the numbers grew and the controversies settled down, organization took over. In many places Pentecostal churches are no more Spirit-filled than any other. As has happened so often before, reform movements end up resembling the mother church.

What is happening now is a revival in the historic churches of the charisms of the Spirit, with a rebound effect on some of the Pentecostal churches. A new thing is going on. Where it goes depends on our constant openness to the Spirit who wants to make us one. We cannot forge ahead of the Spirit, nor can we refuse to go where and how He leads. To become one again will require much openness to our own faults, a willingness to repent of our narrowness, a sincere asking and receiving of forgiveness, and much love. It requires especially a deep love for Christ's Body and a deep conviction that Christ wants His Body to be one.

I hope that no one is offended by the necessarily very brief overview of the growth of Pentecostalism. I am leading up to some perennial problems that charismatics have always had to face. How we deal with them today can very well determine whether this gift of God's new outpouring of the Spirit will yield the fruit of unity or the bitterness of schism. For more detail on the history and theology of charismatic outbreaks see the recommended readings at the end of the chapter.

THE PROBLEM OF STRUCTURE

Surrounding a conversion experience or a release of the Spirit is a community of faith, however vague the awareness of that community may be. The Good News is never announced in a vacuum, but from a particular point of view, with a particular language, and a particular set of customs. We take these languages and customs more or less for granted because they are there and others use them and they seem to be connected with the experiences themselves.

In fact, the languages and customs of conversion experiences or of faith experiences vary widely. Denominational differences represent differences in the language and customs of Christianity. Even the same words have different meanings in different denominations. For example, the word *saved* for a Protestant usually means "having made an adult choice for Christ"; for a Catholic, *saved* means "died and gone to heaven."

These are important areas of consideration, not only because they affect ecumenical efforts, but because they affect the extent to which each of us is open to the full transforming power of the Spirit. A denomination in which the Good News is preached in such a way that people are called to faith in Christ, but not to the baptism of the Spirit, will indeed be Christian; but its members will not be opened to the fullness of the life that Jesus died for us to have. A denomination which does not preach the Body of Christ and the call to community may well have Spirit-filled members, but it will not have the depth of love among its members which God wants for us.

Furthermore, the extent of our transformation in Christ depends so much on the overall community language, customs and structures in the working out of the transformation. People who are used to worshipping in church next to strangers, who are not constantly challenged to love the Body of Christ, these people will *feel* that the call to oneness in the Body is something over and above the call to accept Jesus. When the call to accept Jesus as Savior and Lord is not announced in the context of accepting His Body, then we have God-me Christianity, and everything else is considered to be an extra. One of the major problems we all face today is this "individual" piety. We must all open our hearts to Jesus' call to become one. To choose Jesus is to choose His Body.

TWO BASIC ORIENTATIONS

Another factor which affects the extent and depth of our transformation into Christ is the fundamental understanding of what it means to be a Christian. Rosemary Haughton has done a marvelous study of the relation between conversion and community in *The Transformation of Man*. She points to two basic orientations: "the formation community" and "the community of the transformed." In the formation community, the underlying assumption is that conversion is only the beginning of a saving process which will take the rest of one's life. An example is Roman Catholicism. The community of the transformed operates from the assumption that conversion means one is saved already and now there is only the task of living the new life. An example is Evangelical Protestantism.

The problem we are addressing here is the problem of longevity: how long does the conversion last? How deep does it go? We have an answer in history, because Spirit-filled people in the past have lived through this before. Great Spirit-filled movements have flourished and died, and the people involved were no less Spirit-filled than we are, no less enthusiastic. So, let us beware that we do not repeat their mistakes. Let us not, in the conceit of our conversion, be blind to what the Spirit teaches us from what has gone before.

With her usual deep insight, Rosemary Haughton describes what has happened in formation and transformation communities as they have worked out over a period of years.

If you think of salvation as a once-for-all happening, occurring in this life, you get great fervour, charismatic gifts and behaviour of various kinds (and I don't mean only the more exotic varieties but hardy perennials like charity and peace) and an almost total disregard of ordinary hierarchies and formulations of living, because these don't seem necessary or relevant. But you also get, sooner or later, rigid standards of behaviour enforced by snooping and tale-bearing and harsh punishment. You get, consequently, hypocrisy and empty parade of piety and virtuous behaviour, an emphasis on personal wealth and success, smugness and callousness and bigotry and persecution.

If you think of salvation as something in the future, to be attained by faithful observance of certain rules and participation in certain ceremonies you get humility and hard work and patience and a spirit of service, a respect for authority and for the proper forms of community life, care for others and appreciation of the material things that are necessary for life together and for worship. But you are wide open to minimalism and tepidity, to evasion of personal responsibility and flight from decision. You are likely to be suspicious of anything unusual, to regiment everything and everybody, censoring and flattening all evidence of non-conformity. You get a preoccupation with the communal buildings and possessions, with money and power. And — to make sure nothing is left out of the system — blessings with everything.

(pp. 240 f)

The purpose of all this is only to draw attention to the fact that we all need to be broken again and again in our understanding of what Christianity is about. All of us have sinned. All the denominations have failed in one way or another. We all need to be willing to repent where we have been wrong. We need to be willing to relinquish whatever stands in the road of our hearing the call of Jesus to be His Body.

CONDITION OF MEMBERSHIP

What is often the most difficult problem for people who are newly converted to Jesus or newly baptized in the Spirit is the feeling that their previous Christian formation was worthless and

37

that "ordinary" churchgoers are really not Christians. This has often enough bred "come-out-ism," leaving one's "dead" church to start a new one. Each time this has happened before over the centuries, for some reason the people involved think it is the first time; or they think, "This time we'll live *real* Christianity." But as time goes by, organization sets in and the "real" Christianity becomes just like the old.

The point is not that organization is bad, but that the living out of Christianity requires both the right kind of organizations and the right kind of leadership. Seeing to sound teaching is one of the functions of leadership, and sound teaching will make clear what is required to be a Christian.

Before we go on to Paul's teaching on membership in the Church (the problem goes back that far), I think it would be good to remind ourselves that none of us is perfect. The Christians of our experience are only more or less open to the Spirit. Some speak in tongues, some help their neighbors, some spend a lot of time in prayer. I know "Spirit-filled" Christians who pray in tongues but are on terrible terms with their families and people they work with. I also know "Spirit-filled" non-charismatics who daily lay down their lives for their neighbors. Being a Christian is a matter of being on the way together. The more we see the good that is in others, the more we can rejoice in the variety of ways that the Spirit works.

Paul had a problem with certain Corinthians who claimed to be special Christians because of spiritual experiences. Corinth was a seaport and an international city. Drugs, Eastern mysticism, mystery cults — all these were present there in the midst of the typical pagan immorality. Some of the new Christians in Corinth were also involved in the cults which bred exotic experiences. The people who had these experiences were claiming to be the "real" Christians; and some were claiming that they, not Paul, should be the leaders. Paul responded forcefully in his second letter to the Corinthians:

> We are not so bold, of course, as to classify or compare ourselves with certain people who recommend themselves. Since people like that are their own appraisers, comparing themselves with one another, they only demonstrate their

ignorance. . . . It is not the man who recommends himself who is approved but the man whom the Lord recommends.

(10:12 and 18)

You must endure a little of my folly. Put up with me, I beg you! . . . My fear is that, just as the serpent seduced Eve by his cunning, your thoughts may be corrupted and you may fall away from your sincere and complete devotion to Christ. I say this because, when someone comes preaching another Jesus than the one we preached, or when you receive a different spirit than the one you have received, or a gospel other than the gospel you accepted, you seem to endure it quite well. I consider myself inferior to the "super-apostles" in nothing. I may be unskilled in speech but I know that I am not lacking in knowledge.

(11:1-6)

What I am doing I shall continue to do, depriving at every turn those who look for a chance to say that in their much-vaunted ministry they work on the same terms as we do. Such men are false apostles. They practice deceit in their disguise as apostles of Christ.

(11:12-13)

Please notice that this apostolic community was very, very far from being the peaceful, joyful, power-filled community that we tend to imagine the apostolic communities to have been. Besides the immorality and lack of order and love, there was this problem with false teachers and false leaders.

The Spirit was given to the Corinthians as He has been given to us: so that we might *begin* together the journey of purification. Like the Corinthians, we still thwart the Spirit in many ways by our selfishness and pride, with the all-too-evident results of confusion, factions, openness to false teaching, and all the rest. In the past, ministries gradually developed to see to order and sound teaching, and these are as necessary today as they were then.

Please notice, too, that Paul did not mince words when it came to challenging those who were creating the problems. You can almost hear the remarks flying around Corinth after Paul's letter was read: "Paul wasn't very loving." "He didn't have to be harsh." "Who does he think he is?" We so easily romanticize love into softness and the kind of crippling tolerance which is a betrayal of the Gospel. Paul did not make that mistake.

UNITY THROUGH BROKENNESS

There are today a multitude of differences in theology and worship among those who call themselves Christians. Today the Spirit is doing a new thing. Today the Spirit is calling us back together. Today the Spirit is pushing us to become one Body again. And let us not make the mistake of thinking that it will be easy. It will be a crucifixion, an extremely painful process. It will be absolutely impossible unless we rely totally on the Spirit, which means that we become willing to examine everything in our own feelings and traditions in His light.

We will never become one unless each of us is willing to be changed.

The road to unity will have leaders of all denominations who will be calling us to repentance and love. We must be open to the voice of the Lord from whatever source. And sometimes that voice will be as strong as Paul's in denouncing false leaders and false traditions. Please God, we will have ears to hear and eyes to see. Each of us has been misled and in some ways misinformed — we've got to be convinced of that, or we shall never be willing to look at ourselves in the light of the Spirit. God is doing a new thing! We must pray that He will open our hearts to truth and repentance.

SPIRITUAL EXPERIENCES

So, Paul denounced the false teachers and leaders in Corinth. His own ministry was being undermined, so he continues to defend himself. He speaks of his background and his sufferings, and then he tells of a vision. The point of recalling his vision was that his enemies were claiming visions and spiritual experiences as the basis of their authority.

> I must go on boasting, however useless it may be, and speak of visions and revelations of the Lord. I know a man in Christ who, fourteen years ago, whether he was in or outside his body I cannot say, only God can say — a man

who was snatched up to the third heaven. I know that this man — whether in or outside his body I do not know, God knows — was snatched up to Paradise to hear words which cannot be uttered, words which no man may speak. About this man I will boast; but I will do no boasting about myself unless it be about my weaknesses.

(12:1-5)

Paul contends that he, too, has had spiritual experiences, and there are two important things to notice in this passage. First, Paul had to go back fourteen years to find an experience like this. It was not part of the usual life of a Christian — not even of an Apostle. Secondly, he discounts the importance of such experience. Instead he would boast about his weaknesses; for when he is weak, God's power is evident.

It is not our spiritual experiences which make us Christians or leaders. It is the power of God in our weaknesses. When we empty ourselves out, He can fill us up. When we think we are standing on our own, we fail.

From the earliest days of Christianity, people with special experiences have made the mistake of identifying those experiences with what it is to be a Christian. In fact, we are Christian because we believe and are baptized. Reception into the Church in the early days was a matter of: (1) instructions, (2) profession of faith, (3) exorcisms, (4) baptism, (5) laying on of hands for the Spirit, and (6) the Eucharist. Membership in the Body of Christ, the Church, was not a matter of spiritual experience and judging one's neighbor, but a simple matter of going through the steps above.

Look at the people in your "dead" church. Do you really know where they are with God? Do you have any right to judge?

The first work of the Spirit is to have faith in Jesus. The second work is love. The gifts, including tongues, are given for the building up of the Body, not as proof of holiness or as a reward for holiness. I believe that it is absolutely essential for us, if ever we are to become one, to recognize first of all that the baptism of the Spirit does not make us perfect, and, secondly, that those who have not had special spiritual

41

experiences or gifts of the Spirit can indeed have the Spirit of God.

Once we recognize how weak and miserable we are, even with the Holy Spirit, then we can see that others, too, can have the Spirit but in a different way. I do not mean that all of us are not meant to have the baptism of the Spirit. But I do mean that the absence of this, that, or the other manifestation of the Spirit does not mean that the Spirit is absent altogether.

We are Christians because we believe and are baptized into the Body of Christ. We are all maturing in Christ. We are all growing differently. Let us see the Spirit in each other. What a different experience we would have in our churches if only we would look for the good in each other and rejoice in it, instead of judging one another and putting each other down.

GROWING INTO CHRIST

Finally, let us remember that we are only babies in Christ. Even if we did nothing else for the rest of our lives but seek to understand and live the Gospel, we would still not become all that He wants for us.

The obstacles to becoming the Body of Christ are all that "the world, the flesh, and the devil" stand for. Prejudices, fears, ignorance, bad will, pride, avarice and so much more all stand in the way. As we begin to break down the walls that divide us, we will see both good and bad in ourselves and in each other. Controversies will come. Obstinacy will rear its ugly head. Backsliding will interrupt. Still, the Lord is about a new thing. He will not let us go. For He is building His Body. He is calling us all together in Christ.

> Let us, then, be children no longer, tossed here and there, carried about by every wind of doctrine that originates in human trickery and skill in proposing error. Rather, let us profess the truth in love and grow to the full maturity of Christ the head. Through him the whole body grows, and with the proper functioning of the members joined firmly together by each supporting ligament, builds itself up in love.

> (Eph. 4:14-16)

BIBLIOGRAPHY

RECOMMENDED READING:

McDonnell, Kilian, O.S.B., and Bittlinger, Arnold, *The Baptism in the Holy Spirit as an Ecumenical Problem,* Charismatic Renewal Services, Inc., Notre Dame, Ind., 1972, 53 pp.
Two important essays which bring a lot of clarity to the question: when is a man a Christian?

Haughton, Rosemary, *The Transformation of Man,* Paulist Press Deus Books, Paramus, N.J., 1967, 280pp.
A difficult but rewarding book on the relation between formation and transformation, the role of conflict in transformation. Mrs. Haughton analyzes conflict situations to show the way in which power can break through. She shows better than most the role that community plays both before and after conversion experiences. She concludes with an analysis of the role of the Church in the world. Outstanding.

Delespesse, Max, *The Church Community: Leaven and Lifestyle,* the Catholic Centre of St. Paul University, Ottawa, 1969, 99pp. (Also, Ave Maria Press, Notre Dame, Ind., 1973).
In some ways a difficult book. In every way a challenging book. Delespesse treats authoritatively of the community life of Christianity, what it has been and how it ought to be.

Clark, Stephen B., *Building Christian Communities,* Ave Maria Press, Notre Dame, Ind., 1972, 189pp.
A good book offering suggestions for accomplishing the major pastoral goals of the Church: building Christian communities. Deals with the kinds of principles to be kept in mind.

by Joseph Lange

Growing into Christ 3

We are called by God to be a holy people, the Body of Christ. We are commanded to love one another as Jesus loves us. Our unity in love is to be as close as Jesus is to the Father. In the last chapter we said that it is humanly impossible to live together with all men in love. Only the Spirit can make us one.

But, even with God's Spirit working in us and among us, we shall never be one unless we see clearly how the Spirit wants to work in us. For too many people, becoming Christian or Spirit-filled means becoming "spiritual": learning to pray, getting involved in Bible study, going to prayer meetings. They haven't begun to understand the task, so the task is not being accomplished.

Several years ago a woman I know was sick. She is the mother of several children. A home prayer group went over one Sunday after church to pray for her. One of her neighbors cooked the meals for her. Another neighbor cleaned the house every day. Another took care of the children after school. Another did shopping for the family. Who was being Christian and Spirit-led?

All were, of course. It is important to pray for the sick. But it is also important to help, to work, to do loving things. Many people who become involved in renewal movements or revivals get stuck on the spiritual and never really repent, really change their lives. On the other hand, there are those who get stuck in activism and who never get close to the Lord. Here again it is a question of balance, a matter of including both elements in one's life.

TRANSFORMED HUMANITY

The real task for which we have been given the Spirit is the task of being totally transformed in our humanity so that the Spirit shines through in every way. The Word became flesh in Jesus. The Word is to become flesh in us. When people encounter us, they should be able to perceive the presence of the Spirit. They should feel the presence and power of God, not because of our words, but because of His presence in us. To be totally His, so freely open to His reign in us that others feel it, is the task; and it is not only possible, but something which has happened among countless Christians in the past.

Futhermore, people should also see in us the fullness of humanity in the unique expression which each of us is. The Word is to become flesh in us. Flesh. We become the hands and face and mouth of Jesus. The glory of the Father is that His children turn out all right. The glory of our Father is that we become the magnificent human beings He created us to be, full of love and joy and peace, patient and meek and generous. A follower of Jesus should become more and more splendidly human.

We become more fully human as the quality of our relationships gets richer. We all know how an unloved child turns into an adult who is warped with insecurities and fears. We all know how a loving person can bring out the best in another. Becoming human is not a personal achievement, it is an interpersonal process. The more we love and are loved, the more the best in us grows into fruit. The more we are engaged in life and the more our lives are filled with the wonder of all God's creation and man's handiwork, the richer is our humanity.

In *Friendship with Jesus* we devoted ourselves to building a relationship with the Lord. We will come back to that a little later. Here and in succeeding volumes we want to talk about the other relationships in our lives. If our conversion is to be thorough, if our repentance is to be complete, then all of our relationships must be guided by God's Spirit.

What kind of a human being are you? What are you like to live with? work with? play with? do business with? What do you do that annoys others? How thoughtful and considerate are

46

you? This is the sort of thing which determines the quality of our life together. It is the nitty-gritty of love. It is the workshop of the Spirit.

The Home

Are you a source of peace in your home? Do you make others there feel loved? Do you pray for each one in your family? Do you ask for forgiveness readily when you have been wrong? Do you rejoice in the goodness you see in each member of your family? Do you show them that you do? Do you encourage the others to be themselves? Do you really listen when others talk to you? Are you tender and gentle and warm? Do you forgive easily when asked?

Neighborhood

Do you know your neighbors? Do they find you helpful and generous? Do you pray for them? Do you pray that the Lord will use you for their benefit? Are they glad that you are their neighbor? Do you visit the lonely and care for the sick in your neighborhood? Do you have a personal interest in them?

Friends

Do you share Jesus with your friends? Do you love them without strings? Are you good for them? Do you pray for them? Do you give more than you receive? Do you encourage them to be creative? Can they count on you?

People You Work with

Do you know the people you work with? Have you taken a personal interest in them? Do they trust you with their problems? Do they find you patient? eager to understand them? eager to help them? Are you peaceful and joyful at work? Do you pray for the people you work with? Do you help those who work with you? Do you manipulate them for your own purposes? Do you do little personal things for people at work and so make the environment more loving? Do you pray with anyone at work? Do you pray about your work? Are you honest with everyone at work? Do you do an honest day's work for your pay?

People You Do Business with

Do you take a personal interest in sales clerks, gas station attendants, and others with whom you do business? Do they know that you care about them? Are you honest with them? Do you ever do little personal things for them? Are you patient in lines? Are you fun or at least pleasant to do business with?

The World around You

Do you take time to be present to God's beautiful world, to look at sunsets and mountains? Do you enjoy watching children play? Do you listen to music, really listen? Do you take time to wonder at the beautiful things which men have made? Do you take time to develop your own creativity? Do you read poetry or good literature? Do you ever thank the Lord for all these good things?

Church

Do you know the people you worship with? Have you made any effort to reach out to the needy? Have you ever invited a lonely person or an elderly couple to your home? Have you made friends with the poor of your church? Do you pray for those in your church who are in need? Do you pray for your leaders? Do you encourage and love them? Do you pray for the life of your church? Do you volunteer for any of the unpleasant things that need to be done around the church?

PEOPLE TO SERVE

These questions probe for the things the Spirit does in us to make us one, one with Him and one with each other and one with His creation. If you have ever wondered how and where the Lord wants to use you, you can see that He has put a lot of people in your road to love and serve. You have a lot to do.

I know a man in the Midwest who moved with his family to a small town. The church there was not very alive, so he decided to do something about it. He prayed. He began attending all three Masses each Sunday, arriving early and staying afterwards to meet people. Whenever help was needed, he was there. He did not preach or evangelize. He put his time and energy at the

48

service of his church. In a year's time people were asking him why he was doing this, and that gave him the opportunity to share the Lord. That church is alive now.

I know a beautiful black woman in Chicago, the mother of four. She bakes often, and she always has extra cookies and fresh bread which she shares with her neighbors. Elderly people live nearby too, and she always finds a way to spend some time with them each week. Her children do also. There is a lot more love in that neighborhood now.

One day I was with a small group of women at a morning prayer meeting. One of them was very upset because she was not getting on well with her husband; in fact, the night before he had told her she was a rotten cook. One of the women prayed that this husband might be more understanding. I said that that wasn't the problem. Her husband was right. His wife is a rotten cook. Then we prayed that she might put her heart and soul into becoming a better cook. She did. Now there is more love in that home.

I know a number of men and women who have organized small prayer groups at work. They meet either before work or during lunch. A lot of Christian love is being experienced in those offices now. People in need know that they have friends they can count on.

In our community we run communication skills workshops and growth retreats that deal with bringing the power of the Spirit to our day-to-day relationships. We have watched people grow out of their fears and insecurities into loving, generous people. Jesus is becoming the Lord of our whole lives.

THE TEACHING OF JESUS

As we look at the sayings of Jesus, it quickly becomes evident that His interest is in showing us how to love one another. He came to baptize us in the Spirit; and that baptism is a process, a growth towards the fullness of human life filled with the Spirit.

In the Sermon on the Mount He says, "How blest are the poor in spirit: the reign of God is theirs." We can unravel this saying, as well as the rest, by recognizing that Jesus is trying to set us free. Blest are we when we give up our need to possess. Blest are we when we depend totally on God. Blest are we when we no longer place our security in things.

Once we are poor in spirit, we are more free to be ourselves. We are more free to give love and receive love. We are free to be generous. We are free of anxiety over possessions. We are free to receive correction and guidance. We are free to risk and be creative. We are free to make mistakes. The reign of God is truly ours.

So it is with the other teachings of Jesus. "Blest too are the sorrowing," because God has special love for the poor and the needy. "Blest are the lowly," for when you know your lowliness, you do not expect much from yourself or others. You do not stand on false dignity. You are not the nuisance that a proud person is. "Blest are they who hunger and thirst for holiness," because they can be filled up. They do not have all the answers. They are eager to learn. "Blest are they who show mercy." "Blest are the single-hearted." "Blest too are the peacemakers." These are the things which bring joy to our lives and the lives of others. These are the qualities of divine love in human flesh. These are the descriptions of what it is to be fully human.

Jesus goes on to speak about anger, about having a chaste heart, about divorce, about honesty and oaths with each other, about generous service to others, about loving our enemies, and about doing things from the heart. Jesus does not tell us how to run prayer meetings. He tells us how to live, how to become the magnificent human beings God created us to be. Read the Bible every day. Look for the things that Jesus says about being human. Meditate on His words with the question: What difference does it make to me that Jesus said this? Meditate on the questions posed earlier.

THE TEACHING OF THE APOSTLES

Again, there is no need to compile all that the Apostles have said about how to love one another. Instead, I will pick a few passages and leave the rest to your own Bible study. The thing to look for is how this, that or the other teaching really reveals to us what the Spirit is about: making us into human beings who are growing into the fullness of our humanity, individually and together. It is not enough to pray. We must become loving people.

From Romans 12:
> Your love must be sincere.
> Love one another with the affection of brothers.
> Anticipate each other in showing respect.
> Look on the needs of the saints as your own.
> Be generous in offering hospitality.
> Bless your persecutors; bless and do not curse them.
> Rejoice with those who rejoice, weep with those who weep.
> Have the same attitude towards all.
> Put away ambitious thoughts and associate with those who are lowly.
> Never repay injury for injury.
> If possible, live peaceably with everyone.

(9-18)

From I Corinthians 13:
> Love is patient;
>> love is kind.
> Love is not jealous,
>> it does not put on airs,
>>> it is not snobbish.
> Love is never rude,
>> it is not self-seeking,
>>> it is not prone to anger;
>>> neither does it brood over injuries.
> Love does not rejoice in what is wrong
>> but rejoices with the truth.
> There is no limit to love's forbearance,
>> to its trust,
>>> its hope,
>>>> its power to endure.

(4-7)

Perhaps James expresses it best:
> My brothers, what good is it to profess faith without practicing it? If a brother or sister has nothing to wear and

51

no food for the day, and you say to them, "Goodbye and good luck! Keep warm and well fed," but do not meet their bodily needs, what good is that? So it is with the faith that does nothing in practice. It is thoroughly lifeless.

(2:14-17)

The way in which our faith affects the things we do reveals the fruit of the Spirit. We all come to Jesus mired down in the flesh, and the works of the flesh are: "lewd conduct, impurity, licentiousness, idolatry, sorcery, hostilities, bickering, jealousy, outbursts of rage, selfish rivalries, dissensions, factions, envy, drunkenness, orgies and the like" (Gal. 5:19-21). On the other hand, "the fruit of the spirit is love, joy, peace, patient endurance, kindness, generosity, faith, mildness, and chastity" (Gal. 5:22-23).

HEARTS CHANGED BY THE SPIRIT

We have been saying that our lives in their everydayness will be changed, partly in what we do, but mostly in the way we do it. We should expect our characters to be changed. This is what it means to grow in the fruits of the Spirit. And as we grow and change in the commonplace aspects of our lives, we begin to see more and more clearly the unspectacular side of life in the Spirit, the quiet side. Gradually we experience the deepening of a quiet joy and a quiet peace which convinces us that life in the Spirit is not just a succession of highs, but a bearing of fruit.

These fruits have to do with the daily business of living in a loving relationship with our neighbor. It is in the community and through the contacts of our life together that we are tested and purified in these fruits. These are the virtues of community life in the Spirit.

The fruits of the Spirit are the things that happen in us because our hearts are being changed by the power of the Spirit that we share together in Christ's Body. The Spirit changes our hearts, and because our hearts are changed, our external behavior changes too. The New Covenant concerns the heart, what comes from the heart. The Spirit is given to change our hearts. "The Kingdom of God is within you." Our "hearts of stone" are transformed into "hearts of flesh."

LEARNING TO BE WHAT WE ARE

In one sense, this change of heart is instantaneous; in another sense, the power for change of heart is given and the change takes time. At a Mass some time ago I heard a priest preach on the freedom of a man who has become new in Christ. A sister responded that it was really hard to be free and that it took courage. The priest responded that we already are free, that we just have to claim it, that we just have to start acting that way. As a matter of fact, in the power of the Spirit we are new and free, but we are so used to being in bondage that we don't even know how to behave freely, so we keep on acting as though we are in bondage. A woman said the other day that her husband had told her that if she didn't have anything to worry about, she would invent something! Now she has turned her worries over to the Lord, and she doesn't know what to do with all the spare time! It's like the retirement problem! Anyhow, we are both new in the Lord and learning how to be new.

We are so used to trying to be Christians by living up to external criteria that we unwittingly try to live up to new patterns of behavior which are described for us as typical of a Spirit-filled Christian. We exchange one form of law for another — and we are still in will-power Christianity. Will-power Christianity is a style of life in which a person strives by his own power to live up to some external model or pattern. I remember years ago trying to live like the Saints whose biographies I had read. The result was a host of failures, a lot of guilt and frustration, and a terrible burden. But Jesus said that His burden is light and His yoke is sweet. As a matter of fact, we should live in the expectant faith that that is true. It *is* true if we live from the heart. As time goes by, the Lord will change our hearts and we will do naturally what the Lord is leading us to do at that time. A year ago, "laying down my life" did not include inviting a troubled person to live with me. Today it does.

KEEPING PACE WITH THE LORD

Of course — and let this be noted carefully — I am not saying that we should only do what we feel like doing. What I mean is that we should not try to be more than we are, or we should not try to do things that the Lord has not changed our hearts for. On the other hand, in the basic areas of following Jesus, we are called upon to make choices and to act in specific ways regardless of how we feel. These are the areas of repentance, love of God and love of neighbor. We are to call upon the Spirit working within us to empower us to love God above all else, to act lovingly toward our neighbor, to forgive as we have been forgiven. But then there are special works of loving or praying. For example, it is a mistake to try to live in a household before the Lord prepares your heart for that. For another example, I know many people who today find a great joy in an hour or two of prayer each day for whom fifteen minutes was a burden a year before.

Some months ago I was deeply hurt by a group of people, but I turned it over to the Lord and went about my business. A short time later as I was praying, I recalled what had happened, and I felt all sorts of bitterness and antagonism in my heart. I even began to think of ways of hurting them — it was turning into a great prayer time! I became aware quite suddenly that all this was happening, so I asked Jesus to take the evil from my heart and to give me love for these people. Just like that I felt the burden lifted, and I felt a new love in my heart. Praise God! Jesus really hates this evil, and He really wants us to love; so we can make such prayer requests with great faith. Jesus delights in making us into lovers.

In her book, *Beyond Ourselves,* Catherine Marshall tells of how she decided that since she couldn't stand a certain neighbor, she would avoid her so as not to be unloving. But the Lord kept bothering her in her prayer with the notion that she must love everyone. So she told the Lord that He would have to give her love, because this other woman was repulsive to her. She began to visit with the other woman and to do things with her. In a matter of a few months her feelings changed completely. One day she realized that she really liked her friend!

The point is that we are empowered to love and that we can claim it. Our feelings will follow.

We are making several points, then, and it is important both to identify them and to see how they connect. First, our hearts have been made new and we are free. Secondly, we are already empowered to do what is basic. Thirdly, we are not to expect ourselves to be burdened with the fullness of mature Christian life when we are only beginners. The connection comes in the realization that we are always called to love and forgive, but many other aspects of the Christian life we will grow into naturally as the Lord changes our hearts. This is linked to the realization that the fruits of the Spirit are His work, not ours. Growing into Christian maturity is His work, not ours. You will know when you have bitten off more than you can chew: when you have lost your peace.

Now the fruits of the Spirit, those changes in our character, are the virtues of life in a Christian community. That is the case because it is in the deepening of our relationships with others that the life in the Spirit within us is put to the test, when it is refined and purified, strengthened by fire and given firm roots by troubles shared. It is through the crucifixion of community that the new life of Christ's Body takes on its resurrected form. There is no other way. It is one thing to be joyful at a prayer meeting and quite another to be resentful at being called upon to be of service.

Most important in all of this is to remember that the Spirit has been given to us so that we can endure the crucifixion, so that we can work our way through trials and come out on the other side at a deeper level of love and joy. That is what we must count on all the time. That's why we must never give up.

THE FRUITS OF THE SPIRIT

Now let us look at the fruits of the Spirit. Since the whole next chapter is on love, we will begin with joy.

JOY

Many years ago I was reading the autobiography of St. Theresa of Avila. On one page she was describing the deep joy which persisted even in the midst of exterior turmoil and conflict. I remember thinking to myself that it was silly feminine logic that didn't notice the obvious contradiction. After all, how can you possibly be joyful and in turmoil at the same time? Only after coming into the Spirit did I begin to realize what she meant. Only since then have I begun to experience that deepdown joy which persists even though things are going wrong on a more superficial level. This joy is the fruit of the Spirit.

Basically, joy is feeling, a feeling of exuberance, a zest for being alive. It manifests itself in the smile that is just there, in the desire to sing, in a feeling about the goodness of being alive, even in the desire to shout or to dance. It is exuberance and positive thinking and a sense of well-being. And it is deep. It is a way of being. As with *agape* (love), it is not a reaction to external circumstances; so it remains independent of them. And, again, not being a reaction, it is something which is inside of you. So you can say, "I am not joyful because of what is happening around me, but because I am full of joy."

The manifestations of joy were common to early Christianity and are so to Spirit-filled Christianity today. In many places in Scripture the life of the early Christian communities was described as joyful, and in the liturgy of the Church we are urged to be joyful, to sing and to celebrate. At the 1971 International Conference, Father O'Connor delivered the keynote address on having a song in our hearts. He pointed out how often Scripture exhorts us to sing. Spirit-filled Christians love to sing, even to dance and shout for joy.

As a fruit, a by-product, joy is not something we aim for. It is something which happens to us because we are aiming at something else. This is true of all the fruits of the Spirit. You get fruit by caring for the vine or the tree. You become joyful or loving, not by trying to be joyful or loving, but by seeing first the reign of God in your life. Joy is a way of being human. We begin to experience it as we become immersed in life in the right way. I have been to many parties with people who never heard of the Charismatic Renewal, parties at which someone sits down at a piano and starts a sing-along. Soon everyone is around the piano, singing and laughing and feeling good. For the time being other cares are forgotten, people become simple and childlike and joyful. The world offers this kind of joy, but it is always partial and always temporary. In this way it is similar to the many partial and temporary experiences of being "sound" that every love-experience brings. Each little bit of loving is always experienced as a "salvation." In this case, as is the case with joy, what comes through Jesus is total and enduring.

When Jesus is not the center and not the real Lord, life becomes fragmented, so there are always only partial and temporary fruits. But when we truly choose Jesus as the Way, as the only Lord and Savior, as the primary love, then we become simple and childlike; and because we have given totally, our joy is total and enduring at that very deep level. Then we know why Jesus is the life, and we experience a zest for life.

Joy comes, then, and joy grows as we repent daily and as we seek the Lord first. Deep joy in life comes from loving and being loved. Loving Jesus and being loved by Him brings the greatest joy of all.

PEACE

In John 14:27 Jesus says, "Peace I leave with you; my own peace I give you. I do not give it to you as the world does. Do not be worried and upset; do not be afraid" (TEV).

Each of us is born into the world as a unique person, separate, isolated and alone. This is an element of the basic human condition. As we grow up and are trained to hide our feelings, we develop our own secret inwardness, and our isolation and aloneness intensify. We do not really know each other; and this separateness leads to insecurities, prejudice, fear, and the unloving ways we treat each other — the things which Paul calls the "works of the flesh."

From the earliest time that people have lived together, they have learned to deal with all these fears and inhuman ways of treating each other; and they have done it by establishing laws and customs and good manners. When these regulations are obeyed, a peace is established. It is a real peace, the peace of good order, the peace which the world gives. It is, however, only a partial peace, because it is concerned only with externals, only with how we behave in public. The world does not care about what you really feel; it only wants civility and good order. It even defines "goodness" in terms of politeness and observance of law. Peace, then comes from conformity to a uniformity, and human life is leveled to mechanical common behavior patterns. If one does not conform, he is rejected socially and required to re-form, and this reformation is accomplished by one's own determination. It is all a matter of personal achievement.

The peace which comes from Christ is another matter entirely. What makes the Good News both good and news is that it has to do with the heart, not with external, superficial conformity. Jesus tells us that we are totally known and totally loved: "I know my sheep and they know me ... The Good Shepherd is willing to die for the sheep" (John 10:15 & 11 — TEV). One way of understanding salvation is that we are "saved" from our isolation and aloneness because someone comes to us and offers us himself in love. In this sense, every bit of loving, everyone who loves us, offers us a partial salvation. Through it we are set free from the bondage of aloneness and self-centeredness. But no human being knows us totally; no one knows our whole past and our secret inwardness: so there is always an insecurity in every human love. This insecurity finds expression in the question: "But, if you knew all about me, would you still love me?"

Jesus said: "Peace I leave with you; my own peace I give you. I do not give it to you as the world does" (John 14:27 — TEV). There is a difference between the way the world gives peace and the way Jesus gives peace. It is the difference between living in the light and living in darkness, between life in the Spirit and life in the flesh. If we have not yet experienced that radical difference, then we have not yet begun to experience the fullness of life which Jesus wants us to have.

There is no greater power in human life than love. When a person is in love, loving and being loved, his whole life changes — from within. He is no longer alone and trapped in self-centeredness and self-sufficiency. Now he lives, not just *with* others, but *for* others. His whole value structure changes. He

58

looks afresh at what he is and what he has. This is the great truth of humanism. Love trans-forms: it does not demand re-forming.

So, Jesus comes to each and says: "I know you just as you are. I know you totally, all your secret inwardness, all your past, all there is to know about you. And, I love you. You don't have to change before I love you. I have loved you from the beginning of your life, through every moment of your life. I know all about you, and I love you just as you are. Come, accept my love and return it, and let our growing in love transform you."

Life with Jesus and the Father in the power of the Spirit is no longer a question of externalism and re-forming and conformity, but of acceptance and confirmation and love within. The New Covenant is a matter of the Spirit being poured into our hearts to change our "hearts of stone" to "hearts of flesh." The terrible stifling burden of conformity is lifted and replaced by a loving relationship with God through which we are gradually transformed into His image.

If other loves are "saving," the total knowing and loving of Jesus is totally and eternally saving. It is in this that the peace which Jesus gives is to be found. It is the peace in our hearts which comes from a fullness in our life with God. It's the by-product of being in a right relationship with God. The order which God wants is established and the result is peace.

At a priests' conference which I attended recently, the preacher led us through a meditation after his sermon. He had us imagine that we had been invited to a great banquet being held by Jesus. We arrive at the banquet and are milling around talking to one another. Then, Jesus sees you across the room and starts to walk toward you. You come face to face with Him. What do you see in His face? What does He say to you? What do you say to Him?

As I went through that meditation, I saw in Jesus' face the deepest understanding I have ever known. I knew He understands me, where I am, where I need to go, what I put up with — I knew that He understands. And there was a joy in Him that I was there. He was glad to see me!

As if that were not enough, as I was driving home with another priest, we decided to spend the time in prayer. I just wanted to be quiet and be with the Lord, so I did not say anything. I felt the Lord saying to me, "You are really ugly. You are really one of the most faithless priests I know." Then I knew He understood me. Far from feeling crushed, I felt at the same time His deep understanding and His love and joy in my presence. At that moment I experienced a deeper peace and a deeper joy than I have ever known. It was OK to be me — on the way, not there yet.

I sensed that when I look back from heaven to where I am now, I will realize even more how ugly and faithless I am right now. It is true, and there is peace in the truth when one is loved and understood!

Because of the peace which comes from this primary acceptance of Jesus' love, we are set free from our insecurity and fears; consequently we are able to love and receive love from our neighbor more freely. The love of God and love of neighbor cannot be separated. Because we live in a real loving relationship with God and because we share in His own life, His Spirit, we are empowered to love our neighbor. As our relationships with each other become ordered in love, this adds a further dimension to the peace which Jesus gives.

Still another dimension of the fruit of the Spirit of peace comes from the primary relationship with God. As we grow in trust of His love for us and for all men, as we begin to find the place which He plans for us in His Body, we begin to be content to serve in just that way which He wants, and we are content to leave the rest to Him. Several years ago I remember being very disturbed by all the evil in the world, the hatred and prejudice and killing and fighting, and all the rest. I was really troubled. I began to talk to Jesus about it and I felt Him saying to me: "Joe, I have only a little bit of work for you. The evils you see are my problems, not yours. You just do the part that I ask of you." We can then be at peace about the people we live with and all the rest, concerning ourselves with the task that the Lord assigns us.

Peace, then, is a fruit of the love that Jesus has for us. As

His Spirit fills us more and more, we share more and more in the power to know and love Jesus and the Father as They love each other. We share more and more in the power to know and love ourselves and others as God does.

PATIENT ENDURANCE

Because the world describes goodness and virtue in terms of self-achievement, it also describes patience as an exercise of will-power. The Stoics describe it as a sort of resignation or apathy. People often ask to be prayed with for patience. What they often fail to see is that patience is not something which comes from personal effort, nor is it a "thing" to get like a box of Kleenex. Patience is a fruit, and you only get a fruit when you take care of the plant that produces it.

"Patience" in Scripture means "being faithful to the end," "staying with it until it is achieved." When a short-tempered person meets an obstacle or a frustration, he loses his temper instead of peacefully overcoming the obstacle or frustration. It is not just a matter or putting up with things, but of seeing things in a larger context; in our case, of seeing things in God's plan.

A few years ago I was in a school talking to a woman, a mother of fifteen children. A man came storming out of a bathroom, furious because one of the children had thrown something in a toilet that caused it to overflow. The woman said, "I don't know why you get so excited about that. It happens every day in our house."

Patience is not a matter of will-power, but of values. I'm sure you have all seen some people take in stride what others get angry about. The difference is a difference in values.

Will-power is fictitious. There is no such thing as a distinction between strong and weak will. What that kind of language attempts to get at are differences in the way people behave. But the approach is wrong. One does not build will-power the way one builds a muscle. The power to will is the power to choose. Primarily it is the power to direct one's attention. It means I have the power to determine what aspects of a situation I will pay attention to. If I insist on looking at the irritating side, I will be irritated. If I look at the funny side,

I'll be amused. Using the power to choose is like using a light switch. Whether I bang it down with great emotion or just push it down gently, the result is the same: the light goes on. It is not a question of more or less power, but of the focusing of attention. Consequently, becoming patient is not a matter of repeatedly putting up with annoyances, but rather a matter of acquiring a whole new set of values.

By accepting the love of Jesus and the Father and by being filled with Their Spirit, we partake of God's own life and power. We share in the power to see situations and ourselves and others in the same light as He does. Gradually, as we are gently transformed by His love, we take on His values and we begin to *act* as He does. How patient God has been with each of us! That is to say, He stays with us until His work is achieved in us. He puts up with us; and, knowing how weak we are, He waits and loves us more. As we become more deeply immersed in His Spirit we begin to become like Him.

We become patient, then, not by trying to build will-power and not by asking God for some kind of power called "patience," but by learning to see things as God does. The thing we can do is ask ourselves each time we are annoyed: "Why am I annoyed?" "How does God see this?" In most cases we'll find that we are annoyed because of our own self-centeredness: people are not behaving the way *we* want them to behave, or situations are not the way we want them to be. For example, if we really expect children to act like adults, then we will surely be frustrated and short-tempered when they act like kids.

As we seek first God's Kingdom and are filled with His love, then our whole set of values becomes rightly ordered and we will find that we are no longer impatient. In the passage from Colossians cited earlier, Paul says: "You have been raised to life with Christ. Set your hearts, then, on the things that are in heaven, where Christ sits on his throne at the right side of God. Keep your minds fixed on things there, not on things here on earth" (3:1-2 – TEV).

KINDNESS

To be kind is to be like God. It is a way of loving that

shows itself in a gentle and tender way of behaving. It is the opposite of being harsh. A kind person is also one who does good things for others. He is thoughtful and considerate. Being thoughtful means going out of my way to do something for someone without being asked. Being considerate means taking into account the preferences of others.

We become kind as we relax in God's love for us, as we seek to grow in our relationship with Him. The sharp edges of defensiveness and harshness drop away because there is no longer any need for them, and the life of the Spirit within us impels us to do good to others.

GENEROSITY

Once again we have an example of God's intention to change men's hearts. When a man falls in love, his values change. He now *wants* to give of himself and what he owns to his beloved. There is a change of perspective. Loving has liberated him from a self-centered possessiveness to a God-centered sense of stewardship towards himself and what he has. Sharing in God's Spirit, he becomes empowered to give willingly of his time and possessions to others. Generosity is not a matter of giving a certain amount of time, energy, and money for others, but rather a giving of oneself totally to Jesus. As Jesus becomes more and more clearly the primary love of our lives, then we become more and more God-like, really wanting to help build up this Kingdom of love.

RELIABILITY

The Greek word used in Scripture is *pistis,* sometimes translated as "faith" or "belief." Another possible translation is "dependability" or "faithfulness," which is what it seems to mean here. A fruit of the Spirit is a quality of God's own life, and God is faithful, dependable. Faithfulness is an aspect of love. We really believe that God is faithful to His promises. We count on that. Experience seems to show, though, that we have some trouble in trusting completely. The problem is not that God is not faithful, but rather that *we* have difficulty believing He is. Our trust grows as we find the Lord always being faithful and as others share with us God's faithfulness to them. Gradually our fears and doubts subside.

As a fruit of the Spirit, faithfulness, dependability, reliability grow as love within us grows deeper and more sensitive. We learn how important it is for us to be reliable, that people expect this as a form of love. The whole image of a Body of Christ made up of many individuals performing many services shows us that the interdependence of all the parts only works toward unity when each one is reliable. You cannot have interdependence without dependability. As with God, the only way we can grow in confidence in each other and in the very possibility of the Christian community is if each of us continually experiences the dependability of the rest. What happens when someone fails to mail out announcements, or when someone doesn't show up for that crucial meeting? As the Body matures and grows into the full stature of Christ, its unity becomes more pronounced. This unity is accomplished through the fruit of dependability.

Again, as a fruit of the Spirit, dependability grows as our life in God grows. Our heart changes, and we want to be reliable; we want to contribute to the unity of the community.

GENTLENESS

As with patience, gentleness is often misunderstood. Some think that a gentle person never gets angry. Others think that a gentle person is weak. Some have even taught that a gentleman is one who is well-behaved. If we are to understand what the Lord wants to do in us, we must understand what this word means in Scripture. Both Jesus and Moses are described as being gentle, and both are also described as being angry.

The Greek word means "strength under control." It connotes a lack of violence but not the absence of anger. In a way, anger is perfectly compatible with love. Children need to see their parents angry. It is a way through which they learn the difference between good and bad. Anger is a true human emotion which can be shown to one who loves without fear of rejection.

People are often harsh and abrasive and violent because they are weak. The strong can afford to be controlled. In a gentle person you sense a strength of character, a firmness about what is right. I have often noticed this firmness in those who are full of God's Spirit. Such people are especially easy to spot when they are speaking to newcomers or people who disagree. Paul warns Titus and Timothy not to quarrel or engage in empty disputes over words. I have often seen such people gently share the truth, uncompromisingly and firmly, sure of their ground, yet peacefully and without the desire to impose or control. You can also recognize such people in the way they give correction. Somehow you sense the love along with the firmness.

Such strength and control come from a relationship with God deeply lived. With the full confidence that wells out of the constant companionship of God, there springs an incontestable knowing that one is right. As one grows in the Spirit, so does one's strength increase.

SELF-CONTROL (CHASTITY)

There is nothing misleading here. As we grow in the life of the Spirit, we should expect to grow in self-control, in the control of our desires. As with every other fruit, it is not a matter of will-power, but of God's Spirit working in our lives. Some people wear themselves out by trying to control their desires. They fast and force themselves to all sorts of ascetical practices, and they succeed only in externalizing the message once again. Christianity is about what God does in our hearts first, so that good actions may spring from our hearts. Self-control is not a return to self-centered, will-power religiosity, but a fruit of a life lived in God.

As we grow in the warmth of God's love and are filled more and more by the power of His Spirit, we find ourselves *wanting* to put discipline into our lives so that we will be able to love Him more and so that we might love our neighbor more. We will *want* to get to bed early so that we can rise to pray. We will *want* to fast for a sinner. We will *want* to discipline our behavior at prayer meetings. We will *want* to control our desires for sexuality and food and rest and alcohol. As we seek the Lord faithfully and as He reveals Himself to us more, we will want to please Him more and more.

CONCLUSION

Finally, I think it might be useful to string together some common features about the fruits of the Spirit:

First, they are all community virtues. It is there that they are tested, and it is by them that the community grows into unity.

Secondly, they are not gifts, but fruits; so we do not get them by asking for a gift, but by tending the plant, in this case by seeking the Lord.

Thirdly, the place of personal prayer is affirmed as primary in spiritual growth, for it is there that we "tend the plant."

Fourth, the fruits are not a matter of external conformity, but of inward change.

Fifth, the fruits are not a matter of re-action to external circumstances, but something which happens to our hearts.

Sixth, the fruits are a share in God's own life, in His Spirit. This is what it means to be "holy."

Seventh, the character changes which are the fruits of the Spirit are the result of a radically new set of values which come to us as we yield to the awesome love of Jesus and the Father in the power of Their Spirit.

Praised be Jesus, Christ and Lord!

BIBLIOGRAPHY

RECOMMENDED READING:

Miller, Keith, and Larson, Bruce and Hazel, *The Edge of Adventure*, Word, Inc., Waco, Texas, 1974, 226pp.

An excellent compilation of down-to-earth, practical considerations on how to be a Christian in our everyday situations. Lots of stories and workable principles. Also available with tapes for group use. Don't miss it.

by Tony Cushing

Life within the Church: Agape Love   4

I give you a new commandment:
Love one another.
Such as my love has been for you,
so must your love be for each other.
This is how all will know you for my disciples:
your love for one another.

(John 13:34)

I don't know where to begin. Love? Well, it's everything. It's so important to Christianity that it *is* Christianity. How do you start to describe how vital air is to life? Without it there is no life. Without love there are no Christians; it's literally what makes them live.

The thing we most notice about love is its absence. This is painfully true when you talk a lot about love, as Christians do (or should do). For example, someone once asked Gandhi why he wasn't a Christian. His response was that nowhere else was there so great a distance between a religion's ideals and its practice as with Christian love. Maybe this is inevitable, since the ideal is to love as God loves. But no matter which way we look at it, the mark of the Christian is love.

And Jesus has given us His Spirit of love so that we can be His followers. Then why is it that we don't seem to live this love? Part of the answer is that we have the wrong conception of what love is. Perhaps we were taught a certain kind of love which is impossible to have for everyone. Do we really know what it means to love as Jesus loved?

Before we get into that, we have to answer an old philosophical pun: "What do you mean by mean?"

67

FELT MEANINGS

For most of us, meaning occurs when we connect a symbol with our experience. For example, when I use a symbol like the word *mother,* you understand me by connecting the word to your experience of mother, not a definition. Each symbol or word has a corresponding "felt meaning." When I say "home," your felt meaning might include warmth, security, good food, etc. Your experience is what's felt as meaningful. This is really apparent when you've forgotten a name. "It's on the tip of my tongue." You know it, even though you can't call up the right symbol or word. You know it so well that when people suggest another name to you, you recognize that's not it. It doesn't "feel" right. The same thing happens when you go into your room and it feels different. You can't identify the change, but somehow the room is not the same. Three days later you find out that the picture over the desk is gone. In most of our everyday life, we understand things not by definitions but by the "felt meanings."

The point here is that when you say "love," some people have the felt meaning of romance; others, friendship, motherhood or patriotism. Love means many different things because it means what each person has experienced of love. As we all know, this leads to communication problems. A girl tells a guy she loves him (meaning friendship) and he hears erotic love. A priest preaches love, and people hear love everyone as a man loves his wife. An embrace at the kiss of peace at Mass is mistaken for a pass. And "That crazy kid is in love with his car." Obviously, using the one word *love* to describe so many different felt meanings can lead to confusion.

When something is a very important part of your life, you talk about it in a careful way to distinguish your different felt meanings. When something is not too important, you bunch everything into one word. My grandmother used to call cars "machines" because all they meant for her was a lot of noise that kept her awake at night. But for an auto mechanic, there are hundreds of different kinds of cars, each with its own felt meaning. A Jaguar XKe means something completely different from a Volkswagen bus. We have one word for snow in English.

The Eskimos have over two hundred words for different kinds of snow. Such classifying not only avoids confusion, but also it enriches a person's experiencing of the words. An auto mechanic is usually very interested in cars in general, but he might be ecstatic at the mere mention of a Jaguar.

DIFFERING TYPES OF LOVE

So, one of the first things we need to do is to clarify the way we talk about love. Where do we get our ideas about what love is? What are the different kinds of love?

We probably get most of our felt meaning for love from our parents. This was a very healthy experience if our parents were affirming, forgiving, and knew how and when to let us be ourselves. However, we might have experienced parental love as possessive and conditional. "If you play in the street, Mommy won't love you anymore." "Do you love Daddy more than anyone else?" We might have felt loved only when we were obedient. That might lead us to love others only when they conform to our idea of how to behave. Because of this kind of conditioning, we might think of loving someone who's "bad" not only as unnecessary, but as downright perverse! (We cover this more extensively in Volume III, *Freedom in Christ.)*

Other sources of our ideas about love are our friends, education and culture. In our community we have found that the biggest misunderstanding is that love is basically a romantic or emotional thing. And this is what our American culture advertises. Love is that grand feeling. It is an overwhelming force which buries my reason in a euphoria of sunshine, lollipops and roses. Cliches and songs really point this up. People "fall in love." "Love is blind." "I just can't help falling in love with you." "You made me love you; I didn't want to do it."

There are a couple of aspects of this love American style which put it in conflict with Christian love.

First of all, it talks about love as some kind of *external* force which *sweeps you off your feet.* This is, of course, an accurate description of what it feels like when a man and woman fall in love. This kind of love feels like it's beyond your control, a matter of destiny. So Shakespeare talks about Romeo

69

and Juliet as "star-crossed lovers." Lovers feel that there is something cosmic at work in their hearts. They are destined for each other: a marriage made in heaven. Most of all, it feels like this love is beyond your control.

The second characteristic of the American misconception is that love is primarily an emotion or feeling of attraction. You want to be near someone. You desire to reveal yourself to her. It makes you feel good to do things for her. This is the way you should feel when you fall in love with someone, but it is not exactly the kind of love that Jesus commanded.

Such misconceptions are part of the reason why often we don't try to love others. We feel it's hopeless because *we were taught a certain kind of love that is impossible to have for everyone.* If we think love is primarily feeling good and being attracted to someone, then we feel guilty because we don't have that kind of emotion for everyone. How in the world would you ever *feel good about* or *attracted to* your enemies?

What we need to do is distinguish the various kinds of love that people experience. First of all, this avoids confusion. It also helps us to understand just what it is that Jesus has commanded us to do.

The Greeks had many words to express the different kinds of love they experienced. The most important are:

Philanthropia — This is where we get our English word *philanthropist.* Basically, it means an attraction to union with the whole race of mankind. It focuses on doing good for the whole race and not for a particular person or country (patriotism). Of course, this can be done by a person who loves mankind but can't stand people.

Philia — Friendship; for example, Philadelphia, the "City of Brotherly Love." This love is based on a mutual attraction or union of minds and common experience. *Philia* is simply enjoying the sharing of a common vision and doing things with a person you like. Because of this, it is extremely selective (though not jealous) and always a reciprocal relationship.

Eros — Erotic love. This isn't simply lust. It is the attraction

70

for union with another *person's* body. This is obviously selective (often jealous) but by no means always a reciprocated attraction.

Storge — Affection. This is a general feeling of familiarity and compatibility for someone with whom you have a lot of contact. C. S. Lewis says it's always associated with the word "old." It has nothing to do with attraction or desire for union. It is what students feel for cranky old professors, soldiers for rough commanders ("Old Blood and Guts"), or even what humans feel for animals. Essentially it is growing used to someone and the way he acts (no matter how disagreeable he is).

Agape — What we used to call charity. Agape is God's love, an unconditional way of loving. It is the description of life in the Christian community.

This gives us some kind of a common language to understand different kinds of love. However, understanding what love is and living a loving life are not necessarily the same thing. Most of us discover the power to love when we are loved by another person. To unlock the power to love like Jesus, we need to personally experience His love. Only as we experience, accept and learn the way Jesus loves us, can we love in that same way.

HOW JESUS LOVES US
Jesus chooses us:
> Love, then, consists in this:
> not that we have loved God,
> but that he has loved us . . . .

(I John 4:10)

God reaches out to us. He initiates love by telling us who He is and how He cares for us. He doesn't wait until we are good but commits Himself to us from the beginning.

Jesus serves us in humility:
> The Son of Man has not come to be served but to serve —
> to give his life in ransom for the many.

(Mark 10:45)

71

> But if I washed your feet—
> I who am Teacher and Lord—
> then you must wash each other's feet.
> What I just did was to give you an example:
> as I have done, so you must do.

(John 13:14-15)

In a sense, Jesus gives us His rights. He deserves to be served and loved, yet He gave that up so that He could love us; because of this, we are to be the slaves or lackeys of one another.

Jesus lays down his life for us:

> I am the good shepherd.
> I know my sheep
> and my sheep know me
> in the same way that the Father knows me
> and I know the Father;
> for these sheep I will give my life.
> The Father loves me for this:
> that I lay down my life
> to take it up again.

(John 10:14,15,17)

He suffers and dies to set us free:

> By his stripes we were healed.

(Is. 53:5)

It is precisely in this that God proves his love for us:That while we were still sinners, Christ died for us.

(Rom. 5:8)

Jesus absorbs our hatred and sin. He doesn't retaliate for our evil, but by accepting it He changes us. He is completely involved in our life.

Jesus speaks the truth to us:

He reveals who He is and who the Father is. In love, He tells of our sin so that we can be healed, and He reveals who man really is — a child of God.

He shares his very life with us:

> My peace is my gift to you.

(John 14:27)

All this I tell you
that my joy may be yours
and your joy may be complete.

(John 15:11)

... I call you friends,
since I have made known to you
all that I heard from my Father.

(John 15:15)

Jesus wants to live with us. He desires to give us everything that He has so that we can be happy. He shares His relationship with the Father, and gives us the Spirit and His body in the Eucharist.

He loves us as a bridegroom loves his bride:
On that day, says the Lord,
she shall call me "My husband" ....

(Hosea 2:18)

I also saw a new Jerusalem, the holy city, coming down out of heaven from God, beautiful as a bride prepared to meet her husband.

(Rev. 21:2)

God's love for His people is passionate and intense. God takes pleasure in His people and rejoices over them (Zeph. 3). Sin hurts God like adultery hurts a husband, but He will always take us back. *The Song of Songs* describes the intense longing of God's love for Israel as the joy and hunger of erotic love. This is something of what John Donne meant in writing:
Batter my heart, three-personed God.
Take me to you, imprison me, for I,
Except you enthrall me, never shall be free,
Nor ever chaste except you ravish me.

(Holy Sonnet 14)

THE FULLNESS OF GOD'S LOVE

What we see then is that God's love for us is a complete love. He chooses to create us out of love. He chooses to give us His own life — to save us even though we don't deserve it. He is like a Father to us; so much our real Father that we should say

73

that a loving human father is like our God to us.

> Yet it was I who taught Ephraim to walk,
>   who took them in my arms;
> I drew them with human cords,
>   with bands of love;
> I fostered them like one
>   who raises an infant to his cheeks;
> Yet, though I stooped to feed my child,
>   They did not know that I was their healer.
> How could I give you up, O Ephraim,
>   or deliver you up, O Israel?
> My heart is overwhelmed,
>   my pity is stirred,
> I will not give vent to my blazing anger,
> For I am God and not man,
>   the Holy One present among you.

(Hosea 11:3-4,8-9)

This passage is so emotionally extravagant that God seems almost nostalgic. He is a passionate Father who cares about His children. His love is human to the extent that it is tender and kind. Yet it is always forgiving: "For I am God and not man." The love of a human father, as beautiful as it can be, is only a pale reflection of the completeness of our Father's love. This is the holiness of all man's loving. Our human loves are a "dim image" of God's love for us. Our friendships point to His Friendship, our service reflects His Service. He is Lover, Friend, Father, Bridegroom, Mother, and Brother to us all. Even a loving marriage, when "the two shall be made into one," is a great foreshadowing; "I mean that it refers to Christ and the church" (Eph. 5:32). The reason I'm dwelling on this is that sometimes we get the impression that God's love is cold, sterile and stoical. It's tragic that some people still feel this way. It's tragic that this is actually the way some people experience Christian love.

One reason why people get this impression is that statements we make about God imply a kind of divine indifference. For example:

   — God doesn't need us.

— Nothing we do is good in God's sight.

— There is nothing attractive about us in God's sight.

— God made us to praise Him, not for our sake but for His glory.

— God loves us not because of anything we do but because it's His nature to love.

— We are worthless, and the only good in us comes through God's Spirit.

I suppose that these statements are philosophically and theologically correct. They describe aspects of God which affirm salvation as a free gift, and this we can never deny or water down. However, they give me the impression that God really doesn't want to love us but somehow feels obliged to do so. It's as if the Father reluctantly created us and Jesus begrudgingly became man. It makes me feel as if it were all done so that God would not contradict the principles of His nature. Somehow we have changed a loving Father into a stoic do-gooder. If this pale, sterile, forced charity is agape love, then small wonder few people would want it. It's like saying to a poor person, "I'm only helping you because you're a worthless sinner who could never do anything right anyway."

Yet the living God declares that that is not the way He loves. His love is so rich and full of life that all the intensity, wonder and dynamism of a complete marriage is only a foreshadowing of the way Christ loves us.

If God's love has such human characteristics, then what makes it different from the way people normally love each other? In the first place, our love is the image of God's love in the same way as we are made in His image. We bear a family resemblance which grows greater as we are immersed in the love of that family. So the man who sacrifices his life, even for a wrong cause, reminds us of the Son who "gives his life as a ransom for many." Even a cup of water given to the thirsty is the type and image of the "living water" that Jesus gives.

Of course, we know all too well the fickleness and frailty of our love. Our fears make us wound the ones we love. We give up, fail to forgive, reject the unlovely; and this is in the image of another father, the prince of darkness.

What distinguishes God's love is *forgiveness, faithfulness and freedom.* in the passage from Hosea, God says that He will not be angry but forgive because He is God and not man. Every human has his limit of acceptance. God will always forgive if we ask for it. He is always faithful and constant in His love. He will never turn us away. He continues to love us no matter what we do. "If we are unfaithful he will still remain faithful, for he cannot deny himself" (II Tim. 2:13). Just the slightest touch of this kind of love will change a person's life. This is God's love which is human love made perfect. And all of us are given the power to love in this way which is perfectly human and humanly divine. For if Jesus has commanded us to love as He did, then He will give us the power to do so.

A very good question to ask at this point is: "What is expected of me in order to love as a Christian?" In other words, what is a practical definition of agape love?

WHAT IS AGAPE?

Our community experience has taught us that agape love is basically *choosing to do good* for another person. For me, the best way to explain love is simply to tell some stories about it.

Our first Christian household was accidently formed when a group of students sharing an apartment became members of our community. They started praying for the Lord to use their apartment. In no time at all, there were ten to fifteen people dropping in every night with forty to fifty on the weekends. A few of those who dropped in decided to stay.

One of these permanent guests was picked up hitchhiking; and when we found out that he had been sleeping in cars, we invited him to spend the night. He has stayed for three and a half years. The first three days he spent huddled in the corner, wrapped in a blanket, coming down off a drug high.

It wasn't too easy to be around him. You couldn't understand a word he said because of a terrific stutter. Nor did he seem to be able to understand much of what you tried to tell him about Jesus. He had breath that would kill a horse at twenty paces. He couldn't read; he didn't know how to eat "properly." He leered at women, proclaimed prayer meetings weird and Christians phony. Apparently, he totally lacked the socialization that we were accustomed to. He possessed an infamous pair of tennis shoes, which having been worn twenty-four hours a day for four months, prompted a rapid evaluation by anyone with a nose.

Predictably, we lily-white, middle-class, sophisticated, Pentecostal Catholics failed in almost every attempt to love this person. After a few months, we tried to get rid of him; but he just didn't sense that he didn't fit in. Eventually, one of our roommates, Jim Citro, took responsibility for his upbringing. A few people tried to teach him to read, but that failed, and any attempt to convert him met with frustration. So, he just lived with us.

Little by little, the environment rubbed off on him. The only spectacular thing was that he was healed of his stuttering. Slowly, the love and faithfulness of his adopted father enabled him to go out of himself. For a long time he couldn't hold a job, but now he has kept a job for a year and a half. He started talking to people more. Gradually he joined us in praying, and every night you could hear him talking to the Lord. He stopped taking drugs, not without a few encounters with the police. He still doesn't like prayer meetings; but without anyone pushing him, he goes to Mass three or four times a week.

Now he has become a very other-centered person. He reaches out to the really wounded people he often meets and tries to understand and give some hope. His willingness to spend time with people and to share his possessions is absolutely humbling. He genuinely wants to give what he believes others have given to him. It even gets embarrassing at times when he tells people how willing *we* will be to help them. Just a little while ago, I heard him tell someone that the reason he was still here was "because these guys really love me."

It's absolutely amazing that he believes that, because most of the time we weren't aware that we were loving him. What we felt was a lot of frustration, paternalism and indifference. Gradually a genuine affection did grow, but by and large we experienced a failure to love in a Christ-like way. There were no warm feelings, no big breakthroughs and lots of anger. But somehow he felt cared-for and loved, and I suppose that's all that really mattered.

There were other instances where our attempted love showed no evident results whatsoever. There was one girl who had a life story that sounded like a soap opera. She seemed to feign conversion every three months. Her involvement with the group was a series of deceptions, suicide attempts and freak-outs on drugs. Yet every once in a while she would display a startling generosity and humility that led us to believe that perhaps something good was going on. Finally she was sentenced to a jail term for selling drugs. Even then some people didn't give up on her as I did. They visited her in prison, helped her to find an apartment, got her child back and any number of things. Last reports were that she had straightened out, but I was too skeptical to believe it.

These people were just more explicitly unlovable than most of us. Their fear had worn its way so close to the surface that they were physically unlovable also. They were enemies inasmuch as their presence was a kind of persecution. We've all met poeple who've been hurt this way, and we sometimes fear that we might be this way also. They were completely unattractive in any friendly or erotic sense, and every normal kindness to them demanded a terrific effort.

Somehow stories like these seem too spectacular. They are perhaps the certain demonstrations of love. It's almost success for the sake of truth and justice. People who patiently wait for shy people to open up. Secretaries who smile in the morning and make you feel welcome. All this can be God's love. It can be as undramatic as diapers or as enjoyable as making love, yet still based and rooted in agape love.

Yet, if it can be so many things, what is essential in agape love? It's time to try a definition which is broad enough to describe how God loves us and how we are to love each other.

The most complete and useful description of agape is in St. Francis de Sales' *Treatise on the Love of God.* Father James Finnegan, O.S.F.S., has adapted it to read: *I see good in you and I'm happy for your sake; and I will and act to make your goodness grow, for your sake.*

HOW GOD LOVES US IN THIS WAY

After creating the universe, God "found it very good" (Gen. 1:31). God was happy He created us. And from the very beginning the Father willed and acted to make our goodness grow. He wanted all of us to share in the love He shared with the Son and the Spirit, and He gave us the means to do that. Even after we rejected Him, the Father continued to help our goodness grow by revealing Himself to us in sending Jesus and giving us His Spirit.

Far from being disgusted with us, God has gone to a lot of trouble to help us. Sinful though we are, God is not repelled by us, He pursues us. God is servant, and in Jesus He gives up everything for our sake.

To help you appreciate this more fully, I want to use an artistic analogy. A friend of mine is fond of saying that God made each of us to be a masterpiece. Well, we were in the process of becoming masterpieces and God was happy in what he was creating. However, before we were finished, we were willingly vandalized. And though God was saddened by the corruption we chose for ourselves, He saw that we were salvageable.

Now imagine how an artist would feel if he chanced upon an unfinished Rubens painting decaying in a garbage heap. He would be angry that no one cherished this masterpiece. That's how God feels about sin. He's distressed because something beautiful has been corrupted. But if the artist sees that he can repair the damage and neglect, he's happy because the beauty the creator intended for this painting will be restored. He slaves night and day to renew and complete the masterpiece so that it's better than when it was first discarded. In the same way God rejoices that we are salvageable. He slaves to restore us to what we were before sin and to realize His desire to have us share fully in His love.

HOW WE CAN LOVE EACH OTHER IN THIS WAY

I see good in you and I am happy for your sake.

To see good in each other is the first step in love. It is not

79

necessary to be able to see good *qualities* in the person. A person is good simply because he is a person: he exists. No matter how evil or hopeless a person might seem, we can always say, "It's good that you are alive. Regardless of what you can do for me, I rejoice that you are alive because you can have joy." We do not have to search out the things we like in others. We can be happy for their sake because we know that life is good. Therefore it is good for them to be alive for their own sake. The Catholic position on abortion and euthanasia is based on this kind of love. It is good for someone to be alive, no matter how handicapped he is, because he can always find joy and love.

Sometimes people try to express this by loving Jesus in the other person. This idea of love confuses me. In the first place, there are many people who do not have Jesus in them nor would they want Jesus in them. Secondly, this seems to be saying that you don't really love the person himself, but only love the Jesus in him. Agape love is unconditional: you love *the person* whether or not he has Jesus in him.

Seeing the good in a person is simply choosing to look at him or her in a certain perspective. You can choose to see all the bad things about a person or you can decide to focus on the good. This does not mean ignoring the evil, but rather trying to be like God:

> Not according to our sins does he deal with us,
>> nor does he requite us according to our crimes.
> As far as the east is from the west,
>> so far has he put our transgressions from us."

(Ps. 103:10 & 12)

Seeing the good in a person is more than an attitude. It involves *telling the person about the good you see in him.* This was brought out very clearly once, when our community engaged in a communication exercise which involved telling a person all the good things we notice in him. Afterwards a man commented that we usually associate honesty with telling people their faults or criticizing, and so often we forget to be honest about all the pleasing things we see in each other. Most of the community members admitted that they had rarely told their partner in everyday life what they told him or her during this game.

On the day to day plane, this boils down to being sensitive to the little things in relationships. Very often it's the compliments, thank you's and congratulations that most affect us. "That's a really pretty dress." "It was good of you to reach out to Harry like that; you make people feel very accepted." I try to make it a practice that every time I feel something good about someone, I either mention it or send a card. As our community has done this, there has developed a tangible atmosphere of love and warmth which communicates the way God loves us. "Love does not rejoice in what is wrong but rejoices with the truth" (I Cor. 13:6).

I will and act to make your goodness grow, for your sake.

Agape is a decision to act in another's interest. It has nothing to do with feelings or attraction. If there are warm feelings, fine. They make it easier to love. If they are lacking, then you simply choose to love anyway. As Christians, we have the power within us to do this.

A good example is the parable of the good Samaritan. James Reese, O.S.F.S., says that in one sense the good Samaritan is God, whom we have persecuted and shunned. We are the traveler, wounded and half dead in sin, ignored by the professional religious who are more concerned with ritual than loving service. God overlooks the way we've persecuted Him and then helps and heals us. We should then learn to love as God loves.

To appreciate the extremes to which love goes, we have to understand that the Samaritan helped someone who despised him. A Jew was ritually bound not to talk to a Samaritan in public. John McKenzie says, "There was no deeper breach of human relations in the contemporary world than the feud of Jews and Samaritans, and the breadth and depth of Jesus' doctrine of love could demand no greater act of a Jew than to accept a Samaritan as a brother" *(Dictionary of the Bible,* p. 766). And here Jesus holds up this Samaritan as an example of

81

God's love and the way we are to love one another. The disciples had asked, "Who is my neighbor?" Perhaps we need to ask, "Who is my enemy, that I might love him?" Who is your enemy? Blacks? The Establishment? Hippies? Whites? Your pastor? Your nagging wife or bothersome in-laws? Your boss? Yourself? Maybe even God? You can choose to love even though it's what you least want to do. I can't imagine that Samaritan thinking, "Oh joy, here's an enemy to love." It was probably more like, "Poor guy got beat up. Well, I should stop, but then I've got that appointment. I guess it'll just have to wait. And a Jew to boot — he probably won't even thank me. Oh well, a Jew is a man and he needs help."

Jesus advocated a very practical, no-nonsense kind of love which meets people's needs. The Samaritan didn't sit around and hold the traveler's hand. He did what he could and then went back to his everyday responsibilities. Perhaps he was aware that the Jewish traveler wouldn't want him around. Love meets the other person's needs.

FREE TO CHOOSE TO LOVE

Jesus' command to love our enemies points out the importance of choosing to act for another's interest regardless of what he has done to us. "Love is a direction, not a state of soul" (Simone Weil). We don't walk around full of love. Love is not a thing or an emotional state. To choose to love is first of all to choose to be attentive to another's needs. I can focus my attention anywhere — myself, the past, what I'd rather be doing. Love means I choose to focus my attention on *this person at this time,* right now. Practically, this means listening to this person, trying to understand him. To do this, I have to choose to stop introspecting, choose to forget about my needs, choose to give up the point I wanted to make, the joke I wanted to tell.

I experience this most clearly when I have to choose to ignore my own irritation as I try to love someone. Some people's little mannerisms are a constant crucifixion to me. I always have the choice of what I wish to look at: my irritation or that person's needs. If I remember that most of us are obnoxious when we are most insecure, then I can look beyond the irritation to its source and see a wounded person, not a persecutor. Then I am free not to react to this person's insecurity. I can choose to love him. I don't have to correct his shoddy thinking or tell him to grow up. I can hopefully accept him for who he is. I can choose to look at this person as an equal. He is just as much in need of love as I am.

Practically, then, we can choose to love our neighbor as ourself. Here we see the difference between what we feel like doing and what we choose to do. There are plenty of times when I don't like myself or may even hate myself. I think I'm a failure who always lets people down. However, I am not a helpless slave to those feelings. Sometimes they are so strong that I imagine they are the truth. Most of the time, though, I choose to do good for myself even though I think I don't deserve it. I choose to stay alive, to pray, to accept love and kindness. Even though I might hate myself, I still do those things which will help me to grow. So then, if I can choose to go beyond negative feelings with myself, I can also do that with others.

ACTING FOR THE OTHER'S SAKE

Agape isn't just an attitude of good will. It is acting out that good will in such a way that the other person grows. It might be that my way of loving is not what the other person needs. It is important to realize that we love not just to fulfill an obligation but to help a person to grow by meeting his needs. To promise to pray for someone when what he needs is food mocks love. If a person just needs someone to listen to him, all the good advice in the world isn't going to help him to grow. Imagine the good Samaritan giving the traveler a lecture on how to accept suffering as God's will. And yet these are the kinds of things I see Christians do every day.

I do them myself. The way I want to love people is to sit down and talk with them in order to show my interest in them. However, my roommate's need is that I clean the house. I don't like to clean, I like to talk. However, love isn't for my sake; love is for his sake, so I should just shut up and clean the house.

Some Christians think it's loving to give gifts, when they really should be paying their debts. And generally, at least in renewal groups, people should learn to love by stopping their talk and getting to meetings on time. Responsibility in everyday things is also a matter of love which I find excruciating.

Loving for others' sake means that you are willing to do things that you dislike for their growth. This also applies to tough love and discipline. I might not like to confront people about something they are doing. I would much rather live and let live; yet if what they need is a strong correction, then that's what I should give. Of course, this can be distorted by our tremendous capacity for self-deception. We can easily try to convince people that what they need is what we like to do. Here we have to take the time to find out what people's real needs are and to pray that God purifies our motives.

SHARING WHO I AM AND WHAT I HAVE

In our community we found this idea of sharing to be a good way to express what agape love is all about. Sharing who I am involves letting people know me — my feelings, my relationship with Jesus and others. On top of that, I am willing to take the first step. I go out to strangers to make them feel at home. I start revealing who I am. I share my goodness and weakness with another in case he or she is too shy or fearful.

Sharing what I have is being willing to give my time, my hospitality, talents and possessions if that is what someone needs. It is to place all I have at the disposal of the command to love. How can I love you unless I am willing to give my time for you, to share my home with you?

An important qualification is that we should normally share our selves with a person before we share our goods. Except in emergencies, people feel that sharing possessions and talents is artificial without some kind of personal relationship. The negative feeling the poor have about charity is very often due to dehumanizing "hand-outs." "I'll give you this because you are poor, but don't ask me to talk to you or eat with you or invite you into my home." This is not to say that we should only give when we feel loving toward people. It means that we are willing to accept them into our lives if given the chance.

To wrap all this up, what we need to do is:

1. Choose to look for the good in people.
2. Communicate that goodness to people.
3. Realize we are free to choose to love even when we don't feel like it.
4. Act on our choices and not re-act to people's problems.
5. Love in a way that reaches their needs.
6. Share who I am and what I have.

If this seems awesome, that's because it needs to be balanced by a Christian love of self.

LOVING YOURSELF AS GOD LOVES YOU

Try reading this aloud: "I see good in myself, and I am happy for my sake, and I will and act to make my goodness grow for my sake." Feels selfish, doesn't it? Yet if God loves you in that kind of way, why shouldn't you? Why not choose to see the good that God sees in you? We are cherished by God, and so each of us has to take the risk to believe that *I am important to someone, I am valuable, what happens to me matters.* This can be selfishness, or it can be a simple recognition of the truth about who we are. God seems to have gone to a lot of trouble just so we could believe that He cares about what happens to us when we don't.

A Christian can love himself not only because God loves him but because God loves Himself. The mystery of the Trinity speaks to us of the joy and fullness of God's love for God. God is full of joy in the love of Father, Son and Spirit. In Their joy and completeness is the choice to create so that this joy might somehow be shared and increase outside of God. The Father creates everything for the Son and the Son gives it all to the Father through the Spirit of Love.

Love of self has to do with the reality of our own goodness. We should be able to rejoice in our goodness as an image of the way God rejoices in His goodness. Practically, this leads to doing the things that help that goodness grow. The Catholic Church teaches that a man's first responsibility is to his own salvation.

We should not do anything to risk our salvation. Sometimes this means taking care of ourselves even when we know that there are people who need to be loved. To ruin our health, psychological balance or spiritual life for the sake of others is sheer foolishness. First things first. You can't love others unless you have the power to do that. If you are ill, neurotic or out of touch with God, you just won't be able to love.

So we should balance the need to give ourselves to others with the necessity of making sure that there is someone there to give. We can see this in the life of Jesus. There were times He just had to get away from the crowds and be alone with God and rest. He was a carpenter for most of His life (a waste of time?). He left plenty of work for His disciples to do. When he died, He died for a purpose. He didn't squander His life by "throwing pearls before swine." At least three times people tried to kill Him, but He eluded them because He wasn't here just to be murdered "but to give His life as a ransom for many." He chose to lay His life down at the right time.

We are responsible for taking care of ourselves physically, mentally and spiritually. If trying to love someone is without purpose, more destructive to me than of benefit to him, then maybe I should evaluate my style of loving. We die to ourselves not for the sake of dying, but so that we and others can have life. This points out a greater need to clarify how it is that "the *fruit* of the Spirit is love . . ." (Gal. 5:22) and "This is my commandment: love one another as I have loved you" (John 15:12).

LOVE AS COMMANDMENT AND FRUIT OF THE SPIRIT

It is impossible to love as Jesus does unless we are filled with the power of the Spirit. This Holy Spirit is the Spirit of Love, and the one sure sign of a Spirit-filled person is that he loves unconditionally. As the fruit of the Spirit, love is the result of having our hearts changed by God. Then we can say, "I love you not because of any good qualities but because God has made me into a lover." God is Love, and the more we are open to His Spirit, the more we become a lover like Him. We cannot force this process. It takes time and much prayer. We need to experience God's love every day so that we will be secure enough to love in this way. We need to be healed of our anxieties, our neurotic patterns and our phoniness so that we can love as God loves. The crucifixion of trying to live Christian community and also the love and support that we find there are likewise factors in the creation of a lover.

The result of all this is that we will want to love people. Love will become second nature to us. Perhaps we will even like most of the people we meet. Many of us have felt this from time to time. In the exuberance of conversion or a profound spiritual experience *we feel like loving everyone*. We don't get angry. We laugh at our mistakes and are very tolerant of others' mistakes. People sense our love and respond to this amazing warmth and compassion that God has given us. We become people who create community. Others feel at home around us. We are easy to talk to. We could even pass the Cure of Ars' test of sainthood, which is to listen to a bore for an hour without getting irritated. We are integrated and truly feel that we can do anything with God. Then somehow all that disappears. From enjoying loving people it now becomes a major effort to be polite. Instead of creating community we become a burden to people. Why isn't it easy any more? Part of the answer is that from time to time God fills us with His Spirit to give us a glimpse of what we are going to be like when we are completely open to Him. It's like the preview of coming attractions at the movies. We get a brief taste of what it's all about so that we'll want to see the whole thing. The baptism in the Holy Spirit is the preview of the coming attraction of sainthood. (St. Paul calls it the down payment or guarantee in Eph. 1.) It's important to remember that this effortless love is the result of God's Spirit at work in us. It is not the norm; it can't be legislated or even expected. All we can do is seek first the Kingdom of God and be thankful for the times this love blooms in us.

To be a thoroughly loving person means that God is thoroughly at work in us. We don't have to be perfect — we just have to give God an opening in all our life. More and more as Jesus becomes the center of our lives, all our other relationships will have the right perspective. Agape doesn't take away from love in marriages, friendships or family. Agape helps us to love in all these other ways. There is never any problem with loving certain people too much — in fact, it is probably impossible to do that. The problem is that we don't love God enough. I'd like to diagram this so that it's really clear:

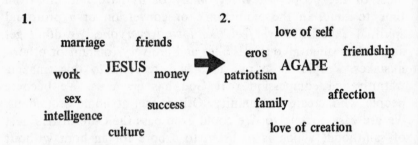

1.

marriage   friends

work   **JESUS** money

sex   success

intelligence

culture

2.

love of self

eros   friendship

patriotism **AGAPE**

affection

family

love of creation

Loving God and being open to His Spirit   leads to   **becoming a loving Person.**

Seek first the Kingdom and all else will follow.

1. Putting Jesus at the center puts everything in the right perspective. The fruits of the Spirit are evident in all our relationships and endeavors.

2. Agape becomes our basic relationship to all people. This gives the right balance and perspective to all the other kinds of love.

Again, this takes time, prayer community and daily repentance so that we become this kind of a person.

LOVE AS COMMANDMENT

It seems almost impossible that Jesus would command us to love in the kind of way I have just described. But we also have the right to expect that if God commands us to do anything, He will give us the power to do it.

What then does this commandment involve? It means that

we are always ready to *forgive*. "Love does not keep a record of wrongs ... Love never gives up, its faith, hope and patience never fail" (I Cor. 13:5-6 — TEV). We can always be willing to give people another chance. This is within our power. What God commands is that we choose to do good for others no matter what we feel, regardless of what they do. This is within our power. We can't control our feelings. We can't psych ourselves up to like people. We can choose to see good in them. We can choose to do good for them. We can choose to forgive them, pray for them, talk to them and share what we have with them.

The amount of what we can do for people grows as we are transformed by the power of God. We are commanded to love to the degree that God has given us the power to love. All of us already have the power to forgive and to choose to do good for people. Gradually we will have the power to share our homes and our possessions. Again, it helps to see this in a diagram.

Commandment	Commandment	Commandment
forgive	forgive	forgive
do good	do good	do good
	listen	listen
	share who I am	share who I am
		share what I have
		invite people to live with me
		go out to the poor and weak

As our freedom and power grow, our responsibility grows also. What happens is that trying to follow the commandment to love opens us up to the Spirit so that we are transformed into loving people. Expending effort, working out the discipline and formation of the command to love leaves us vulnerable to the Spirit who produces in us His fruits. By struggling and choosing to do good, we eventually want to love as Jesus loves.

AGAPE AS COMMUNITY

Agape as a mutual relationship is only possible among

Christians because the Spirit can lead people to love this way. For Paul, agape becomes the atmosphere of the Christian community. In a sense agape is the definition of the Christian community. We are to be rooted and grounded in love (Eph. 3:17). Love is the basis of all ritual and action. We are bound together in love. *Christian community is the relationship of agape love to one another.* Without this love we are only a mob. With agape, Jesus is present. His Spirit dwells with us and in us. Agape is community. Community should be agape. There is absolutely no way we can claim to love God without loving our brother. In fact, we love God as much as we love our worst enemy. The two great commandments are completely joined together. We love God *if* — and only *if* — we love each other. We can love each other *if* — and only *if* — we love God.

Dear friends! Let us love one another, for love comes from God. *Whoever loves is a child of God and knows God.* Whoever does not love does not know God, because God is love.

God is love, and whoever lives in love lives in God and God lives in him. This is the purpose of love being made perfect in us: It is that we may be full of courage on Judgment Day, because our life in this world is the same as Christ's.

We love because God first loved us. If someone says, "I love God," yet hates his brother, he is a liar. For he cannot love God, whom he has not seen, if he does not love his brother, whom he has seen. This, then, is the command that Christ gave us: he who loves God must love his brother also.

(I John 4:7-8, 16-17, 19-21 — TEV)

Beloved, let us give our lives to this.

BIBLIOGRAPHY

RECOMMENDED READING:

Fromm, Erich, *The Art of Loving,* Harper & Row, New York, N.Y., 1956, 118pp.
This famous psychoanalyst's insight into the qualities and practice of the different loves is most compatible with a Christian perspective. Thoroughly excellent book in every respect except that the chapter on love of God is very vague.

Kierkegaard, Soren, *Works of Love,* Harper & Row, New York, N.Y., 1962, 378pp.
This is a most thorough and profound collection of discoveries on Christian love by this famous 19th century theologian-philospher. It is a reflection on the two great commandments to love God and neighbor and I Cor. 13. A very challenging book, though some might have difficulty with the style.

Lewis, C. S., *The Four Loves,* Harcourt, Brace, Javanovich, New York, N.Y., 1960, 192pp.
Lewis, wise after many years of attempting to love, describes the different kinds of love with a simplicity, honesty and wit that both enthralls and challenges us. The only flaw is that the chapter on friendship is much too clubby and highbrow and lacks practical advice on Christian friendship. Nevertheless, I found this the most enjoyable book on the nature of love.

Powell, John, *Why Am I Afraid to Love?* Argus Communications, Niles, Ill., 1972, 120pp.
Easy to read, insightful combination of modern psychology and Christianity. This is very good for understanding the everyday fears and defense mechanisms which are obstacles to mature love.

by Tony Cushing

Christian Friendship 5

We are to love one another as Jesus has loved us. Does this mean that everyone has an equal claim on our time? If agape love is not necessarily being attracted to someone, what place does mutual attraction have in community? Is there a place for intimacy in community? Answering these questions is the goal of this chapter. Since this whole topic is often neglected, I want to explore in depth the advantages and problems of Christian friendship.

NEED FOR FRIENDSHIPS

Human beings usually have a deep need for intimate loving relationships. And Christians (most of whom are human — though a few try to deny it) share in this God-given need for intimacy and companionship. Even Christians who belong to enthusiastic, faith-filled communities still seem to have this need. Now, by need I do not mean a compulsion or deficiency, though it can be that at times. An authentic need is something that helps people to grow and be more human. Men need to pray, to love and be loved, to relate to nature, to be creative, to play; and to recognize these needs is a sign of strength and wholesomeness. The ways intimate friendship can help us to grow are obvious: we are known and loved for who we are; we feel there are enjoyable, likeable people, and, because of this, we can simply relax and have fun with our friends. For Christians this is simply to take seriously in all it's implications the first statement God addresses to man's needs: "It is not good for the man to be alone" (Gen. 2:18).

In terms of the everyday life of Christian communities, this is merely a matter of common sense. If there are more than ten or twenty people in a group, it is impossible to know all of them intimately. First of all, you just don't have the *time* to do that even if you spent all day at it. Secondly, you usually don't have the *psychological energy* to get to know more than two or three people really well. When I've overdone it, I usually get emotionally exhausted and end up being unable to relate to anyone.

We have to face the fact that our time is limited. We have only a certain amount of energy and emotional involvement to give. To deny this is to court a variety of breakdowns. Last of all, and perhaps most importantly, many people will probably not want to be your friend in an intimate way. Neither will you want to be intimate with them. You simply don't have much in common. You don't enjoy this person's company, and the feeling is usually reciprocal. Now, you can still love each other; but when it comes to making a choice about how to spend your time, you will naturally choose to be with someone you like, someone who likes you. There are a number of qualifications, but this generally seems to be the way we humans are.

This has been our community experience over the last four years. The reason for this chapter is that we have found close friendships to be a tremendous aid to our Christian growth. That wasn't always the case. In the exuberance of conversion, we ignored many of the everyday facts of life like friendship. For a while, people somehow felt that to love everyone equally they had to give everyone an equal amount of time. After that, we tried to structure intimacy. We tried to get everyone to commit himself to a weekly small group prayer meeting. That was a good idea; it made all kinds of sense — except that it never worked. People just didn't share deeply with people they didn't like. It felt artificial. It was artificial. Because of this experience, we reexamined our life and decided that the need for intimacy could be met more easily and more fully be developing spiritual friendships. There are problems with this, but by and large it works for us. A structured small group experience can and does succeed for other groups. They give witness to how the Spirit works in that way. We can't. We can only speak of what we have seen and heard the Spirit doing in our own lives.

It is obvious and inevitable that people (Christians or not) will form intimate friendships. The task now is to discover how we can be friends in Jesus. But before we can do that, we have to look at the more basic question of what friendship is.

WHAT IS FRIENDSHIP?

In a sense, everyone who has ever had a friend knows what friendship is. At least he knows what it feels like, even if he couldn't define it or even describe it. Now the problem is that many have never experienced a close friendship. And there are many more who experienced a kind of diluted friendship with people at work or in the neighborhood. These are the folks who have "lots of friends." I suppose that what they mean by "friends" are people they can talk with for half an hour without getting into an argument. This is not to say that these people are wrong. They are just being misled about the quality of their relationships. It's like giving someone ginger ale and calling it champagne. He might have suspicions about what he's getting, but he doesn't know what he's missing until he tastes the real thing.

Much of this lack of friendship springs from the particular insanity of the American life-style. We don't waste time on people. We mass-produce acquaintances and end up knowing no one — least of all ourselves. A lonely nation too much on the move to be tied down by commitments. Obsessed with achievement, we can't enjoy each other as gifts. And if we should judge a man by the company he keeps, what rating would a TV set get?

If I sound a bit too pompous or self-righteous, it is just that I have experienced so much joy and growth through my friends that it irks me to see friendship being phased out by the American mania for busyness. I have been greatly blessed with beautiful, loving friends. They are God's special gifts to me. They have challenged me to grow out of my phoniness. They have put up with me at times when I couldn't even stand myself. In them I have seen and touched the love and mystery of God in the love and mystery of human beings. They have most graciously helped God in the wild process of creating me to be His son. And most amazingly, they have kept me sane most of the time, which is no small accomplishment. And so I'm writing this chapter with an ulterior yet benevolent motive: I want everyone to be able to share in the great joy I have in those who have blessed me with their friendship.

To get back to what friendship is, I would say that it's basically people who enjoy each other, have the same vision of what life is and choose to share their life together.

ENJOY EACH OTHER

Most Christians understand that loving someone is not necessarily liking someone. Jesus commands us to love everyone and gives us the power of the Spirit to do just that. Trying to do it for just a short time convinces us that Jesus has not given us the power to *like* everyone. We find that trying to love certain people is tantamount to being persecuted. And if we're graced with humility, we soon learn that our idiosyncrasies give others the chance to "do good to your enemies." This is agape love at its most heroic, but it is not what we are talking about in friendship.

Friends are few because there are few people whom we like to be around and who like to be around us. You like to talk to them. You enjoy their humor, their spontaneity, their seriousness; and they enjoy similar things in you. Most of all, *you enjoy doing things together.*

A friendship usually isn't focused on the people involved but on something they share together. Romantic lovers stand gazing into each other's eyes, but friends stand side by side to look at and enjoy something outside themselves. You discover that there's someone else who shares your passion for ideas, skiing, collecting, poetry, warfare, and Christian community. Any kind of an interest, as long as it's shared, can lead to a friendship. Friends support your interests and desires. They tell you that you are not alone in what you see life to be and what you think is worth doing. This can be a good thing, like sharing a passion for ecology and preserving the beauty of nature; or it can be an evil thing, like sadism or a shared hatred of a particular ethnic group. Either way you find that you are not alone because your friends tell you that this is the right way to see things. So you have a group of friends gathered around Jesus or Augustine or Ralph Nader, and then you have the friends of a Marquis de Sade or a Hitler. Either way the dynamics of a shared vision work to support us in our idiosyncrasies.

I experienced this most clearly in the group of friends from my college. We were the underachievers. All of us were intelligent scholarship boys who shared a cultured, liberal, yet cynical and pessimistic view of education, society and the cosmos. We all loved good music, good books, witty conversation, manic depression and procrastinating. There were secondary interests of ping-pong, pacifism, pornography, suicide and unrequited love. Above all, we really cared for each other, rejoiced in each other's success and groaned together in epic undergraduate depressions. These men taught me what love was and saved me from at least one serious attempt to take my life (not to mention a few humorous attempts). And after knowing these people, it was very easy to understand what a loving community was supposed to be like.

Yet there were problems. We affirmed each other's sickness as well as sanity. There was the tendency to snobbishness that is the danger of every group of friends. It's not that we actually thought we were superior. It was just that we saw the truth of what life really was, and it was absurd. Other people, less courageous, less intelligent, could be happy in their ignorance; and we tolerated this in the same way a pompous priest might wink at the lust and drunkenness of his congregation. We were the keepers of the secrets of the cosmos, and it was a dark yet noble burden. Because of this existential snobbery, we didn't really help anyone outside our little circle. Also, since happiness and sanity were a kind of cosmic faux pas, we actually encouraged each other to neurosis and failure. This is what often happens to friendship without the love and power of God. It was wonderful, yet it lacked something to make us whole and healthy people. What it did was eventually to make this group of agnostics more aware of the emptiness that only God can fill.

The reason why I took such a long time to describe this purely secular friendship was that it is the best picture of the strengths and weaknesses of friendship in general. Also it frees us from the naive notion that only Christians can be real friends. Far from being evil, the love and goodness of those men formed me for the greater love and goodness of God. Since about half of the group has now entered our community, we can clearly see the difference that Jesus has made in our lives. Even though we are far happier, the friendship is less intense and in some ways more difficult now. The reason is that we have far less time for each other, and we probably don't need each other as much as we used to. If anything, Christian community has caused problems to our friendship, but then we are more honest now and challenge each other a lot more. And most amazingly, we've seen that God can get us through the darkest, most wounding experiences of each other, and that gives us a stouter hope.

HOW FRIENDSHIPS HAPPEN

Thinking back to the beginnings of that college group, I would have to say that friendships come about spontaneously. You find friends or discover them with delight. We are always surprised to find someone who sees things the way we do. The question of friendship is, "Do you like the same things?" It's finding someone who seems to understand you even if he or she hasn't spent a lot of time with you. As John Powell says, it's the quality of communication which determines the depth of the relationship. You can spend years with someone and never have a friendship, or you can find a friend in one evening's discussion. Spending time together doesn't create the friendship, yet once the friendship happens you have to spend lots of time together.

This means that you can't structure friendship into community life. If you search for a friend, you probably will never find one. It's a matter of focus. *Friendship happens because two people see the same things in life; and, as an indirect result of that, they find a friend.* There is nothing more alien to friendship than one asking another to be his friend. It's like asking somebody to fall in love with you or telling someone to make you laugh. Doing that focuses your attention on yourself: "Be *my* friend, make *me* laugh." And nothing inhibits joy or friendship more than self-centeredness. Friendship reveals the Christian principle of dying in order to live. If you seek your own friendships, you'll never find them; but if you seek what you enjoy and be yourself, friendship will happen.

I can't stress this enough because so many people get hurt expecting others to be their friends simply because they are in the same community or spend time together. It's almost as if the people who most need friends never find them. They desperately want to have someone like them, to be enjoyable and special to someone. Very often they are insulted by agape love and subtly demand that they be liked for their own good qualities. This is manifestly impossible to do. You can't turn friendship on and off like a light switch. You can choose with the power of the Spirit to love someone, but you can't simply choose to like someone. Friendship is very often determined by things we can't control — environment, education, intelligence. The very idea of stamp collecting is a bore for me, but for others it's the zestiest thing in life. In turn they might think that my classical music is only useful as a cure for insomnia. For us to try to force a friendship, to pretend to enjoy what we abhor, would be a tremendous waste of time.

So, as to creating friendships, the only thing you can do is to pray, be yourself and wait for people who enjoy you and whom you enjoy. For some people this will take a while; for others it happens quite easily. Part of the reason is that some of us have been so crippled by the world that we aren't very lovable or enjoyable people. All of us are unlovable in one way or another, but there are some who have been so wounded that they have never gone out of themselves, never developed talents or hobbies, who find life a bore and consequently are a bore to others. It's almost impossible for these people to find friendship until they are healed enough to have a capacity for joy. I say *almost*, for there is often a friendship of despair where people share their suffering and in the mutual darkness find a kind of light. It is the glory of a Christian community that these people find love and acceptance from Christians who might not really like them yet lay down their lives for them in love. Christians can't give friendship to everyone, nor should they try. Instead, their promise is, as the song goes, "I can't give you anything but love."

FRIENDSHIP IN CHRIST

It seems that people just naturally develop friendships, and friendship is essentially selective. The big question is, how can our friends bring us closer to God? How do we integrate the dynamics of friendship with the command to love all people equally? Can we fit this natural attraction into the greater scope of God's love? To answer is to discover what is essential in Christian friendship and what distinguishes it from other kinds of friendship. What we have found as an answer is that Christian friendship should include *sharing, witnessing, accountability* and *prayer.* We borrowed this from a Cursillo priest. As an anagram it spells SWAP, which is good for a memory aid, but often has the wrong connotations.

SHARING

Sharing is first of all letting people know who you are so that a friendship might evolve. It means communicating your "gut-level feelings," what you like and dislike, letting your friends know what's happening to you. In marriage, households and intense friendships this will most often be a daily reporting of what's going on when you are not together — sharing what happened at work, who you talked to, what you've been reading. There is more to this than communicating information. It is communicating *feelings* more than beliefs or information. (We deal with this in more depth in our third volume, *Freedom in Christ.)* Maybe we felt guilty about something our boss said to us or threatened by someone's success. This new book made us realize that we were wrong about something and we feel rather stupid. The reason I mentioned only negative feelings is that most of us are usually willing to share our joy and goodness. Sharing is being able to let another know us in our weakness as well as our strength, to know our sinfulness as well as our love. This is the tremendous risk of all friendship. We are vulnerable to another. We let them know what hurts us. We give them power over us because we trust them to love us even when we know we're unlovable. For a Christian this means trusting that the other person loves you with God's love over and beyond his friendship with you.

This day-to-day sharing and defenselessness is probably the hardest part of friendship. It takes a lot of time and energy to break down our tendencies to externalize and peel off our masks of goodness. It is precisely here that friendship is so important. Our friends will challenge us to share. We can't be phony with our friends. If we put on a show, they're more likely to say, "Knock it off; what's bothering you lately anyway?" And if we know that they really know us, then it's easier to avoid becoming a sham.

Because it's so easy to hide ourselves, it is often necessary to have a structured time of sharing between friends. The idea here is that there are bound to be spells when we don't feel like telling people who we are. So, since we don't trust ourselves to want to do this, we structure it in. This is to make explicit that we consider the friendship more important than the demands of either our moods or our busyness. It also means we have to take time to share ourselves; otherwise the friendship will die. Maybe you call every day, or have lunch, or play golf once a week, what's important is that the structure challenges you to share in a regular way.

The greatest killer of friendship, as of marriage, is non-communication. My most common form of non-communication is simply not wanting to bother someone else with my problems. Underneath this is a real aversion to letting someone experience me in my weakness, a fear of depending on someone's love. Of course I give it an acceptable motive like, "They're really too tired," or "They don't have to hear this from me." If I'm angry at them, it's "Well, I'll let it blow over; it's too much trouble to get into an argument over." Thank God, my friends won't put up with that when they sense that I'm upset about something. They'll bug me till I tell them what it is. It also happens that it's very easy to read my feelings.

When I'm happy, I smile and sing a lot; but when I'm sad I look like a lost puppy. This transparency is often a blessing but seems a curse when I merely have a headache and everyone tries to help me out of my depression instead of letting me take an aspirin and a nap.

This sharing of who I am, essential as it is, is probably not the major part of what most friendship is. The real occupation of friendship is doing things together, sharing what you like to do, enjoying things together. Whether it's books, nature, music, games or whatever, just having fun enjoying these things is what friends probably spend most of their time doing together. And it is a great work of the Spirit of God that people can relax and be re-created together. It's wonderful that even Christian friends can get together and laugh, because the laughter is so often directed against our own self-importance. We really can't take ourselves too seriously in the midst of people who know us well. We can enjoy our mistakes, kid each other about our faults in a kind of mock aggression which is a lot like tickling. The loving laughter of friends quickly kills any pretense to self-righteousness; and, because we are so accepted, we can even laugh at ourselves. As to the holiness of laughter, they say that the first group of English Franciscans could hardly keep from laughing every time they looked at each other. I think this was not only from great joy but perhaps from an even greater humility.

WITNESSING

Witnessing is simply sharing what God is doing in your life. This is different from sharing who I am. Witnessing builds faith; sharing builds the friendship. You can have a friendship without witnessing or prayer, but it probably won't be what I would call a spiritual friendship. What Christian friends understand as most essential to life is their relationship with Jesus. They realize that the best thing they can do for the other is to help that person be holy.

Most enthusiastic Christians (evangelicals, Pentecostals, charismatics, etc.) understand this very well. In fact, when I travel around to different prayer groups, I find that very often the problem is that some Christians consider witnessing the only way two people can and should communicate: constantly talking about Jesus may actually inhibit getting to know each other. I can hide behind religious language and pious stories just as easily as I can hide behind anything else. What can happen is that even though people meet together often to pray and talk about God, they never feel that anyone really knows them and loves them for who they are. Often they end up feeling isolated. What is needed then is not more prayer but a lot of down-to-earth communication. Perhaps you might be thinking that I'm implying that prayer isn't enough to build community. Well that's exactly what I am saying.

Witnessing, however, is vital yet most traditional Christians haven't been taught that talking about our relationship with God is part of a normal Christian life. This is especially true of our prayer life. Somehow it seemed against humility to talk about how you experienced God in prayer. This bred a nagging suspicion that maybe people experience nothing in prayer or don't pray at all. The subject is almost a taboo among most Christians and usually causes great embarrassment. As a seminarian once told me, "Asking someone how his prayer life is, is like asking about his sex life." Nowadays, it seems that at least some Christians are more willing to talk about sexual than religious experience.

If a Christian professes to love God with his whole heart, mind, soul, and strength, then how can you really know him unless you know a good deal about his relationship with God? We need to share the good things God does for us to help each other have faith in His love. Discussing theology or helpful books and trying to overcome doubts is all part of friendship in Christ. Most of all, I would think it important to talk about our prayer life and our attempts to love and serve our brothers and sisters. Very often just talking about problems in prayer with a friend can help us to solve them. Friends can be more objective, and perhaps they have experienced the same kind of problem and can help us get out of it. Also it helps in knowing how to relate to someone if we know that he or she is going through some kind of dark night in prayer.

Keeping in touch with our friends' relationship to God helps us to be more flexible in responding to their needs as they pass through different phases of their Christian life. When someone is going through insecurity or darkness with God, it usually is not a good time to challenge him to holiness or to expect warm, affectionate love. This happened to me recently when I was in a prolonged dry spell in prayer. I went to a party, and my closest friend asked how the day was. I grunted something ambivalent and proceeded to ignore her throughout the rest of the evening. The result was that she felt terribly rejected because she had no way of understanding that my reaction was from weakness and not a comment on how I felt about her. Had I been honest about the aridity of my life with Jesus, she would have known how to respond, and a lot of hurt would have been avoided. Our community has found it helpful to "check in" — to report our feelings and how things are going with Jesus as soon as we see each other.

For people who become friends after both are already explicitly Christian, witnessing is usually very easy. However, I found that witnessing comes harder with people who were friends before they were Christian. The reason for this is that Christianity feels awkward and added onto the friendship, and it is. They already have a comfortable pattern of relating together which works, and that is hard to change for any reason. Friends feel that the "old man" is more real than this new Christian overlay. It takes a while for the new creation to reach the innermost depths of our personality. There is a danger here of giving in to the "old man" and simply leaving God out of the friendship. Eventually, however, this makes the friendship alienating, since we can't share what is supposed to be the core of our lives. A second danger lurks in our feeling so at home around old friends that we're comfortable in being our-old-self-the-sinner and fail to be challenged to grow. We must stay aware of the necessity of witnessing to each other, to make it an explicit part of our relationship so that ours becomes a friendship of faith.

ACCOUNTABILITY

I am responsible for the one I love.

(The Little Prince
by Antoine de Saint Exupery)

O how much more doth beauty beauteous seem
By that sweet ornament which truth doth give!

(Shakespeare, Sonnet LIV)

If thy unworthiness rais'd love in me
More worthy I to be beloved of thee.

(Shakespeare, Sonnet CL)

Everyone has enough bad inclination of his own without
burdening himself with another's. Far from requiring this,
friendship obliges us rather to aid and assist one another to
free ourselves from every kind of fault. We must of course
put up with a friend's fault, but we must not lead him into
faults, much less acquire his faults ourselves.

I speak only of imperfections. As to sins, we must
neither occasion them nor tolerate them in our friends. It is
either a weak or sinful friendship that watches our friend
perish without helping him, that sees him die of an abscess
and does not dare to save his life by opening it with the
lance of correction.

(Introduction to the Devout Life,
Part III, No. 22, pg 183)

Am I my brother's keeper?

(Cain, Gen. 4:9)

To be accountable is to take seriously the responsibility of
challenging each other to grow. This entails encouragement as
much as correction, honesty about each other's goodness as well
as each other's failings. In our community, I've seen people grow
only when they are loved and affirmed by the Lord and by His
people. As we feel more and more secure in being loved, we can
begin to face the sinfulness in our lives. This seems to be the
way Jesus loves us. He convicts us of a few big faults in our life

105

at first and then *gently* brings out our other flaws over a period of years. If God convicted us of all our sinfulness at once, we would be psychologically and spiritually shattered. Perhaps it is because most of us have such a poor image of ourselves that criticism often causes more problems than it solves. Many of us have been severely hurt by the negative judgments of our parents and teachers, and consequently a slight admonishment can often reopen all the old wounds. Our feelings of worthlessness and guilt act as barriers between God and the majority of us. *We probably need to be healed and affirmed in love before we can grow by means of correction.* To accept a correction made in love, we first have to experience the reality of the other person's love for us.

For me, this means that I accept correction from my friends more readily than I do from anyone else. If I feel that someone is censuring me just because I'm not obeying a law or because my behavior isn't up to his standards, I get defensive and usually don't listen. However, if someone who knows me says, "You might be a lot happier if you tried doing this," I feel that the correction is intended for my growth and is given in love.

I try to avoid talking about past mistakes and concentrate on what can be done to change things in the future. For example, I have a bad habit of isolating myself whenever I get depressed. This is a stupid way to solve my problem, and I know it. Nevertheless, if someone were to point out how futile it is, how bad for the community, I'd probably sink further into depression. A friend once told me that in the future, whenever he spotted me acting that way, he would spend time talking with me so that I could break the pattern. He told me this at a time when I wasn't depressed, and I agreed that he had a good idea. However, the next time I got depressed I thought it was sheer foolishness (I hate to let people see me weak), but the fact that this person weathered all the abuse and silliness I threw at him was proof to me that he was doing this out of love, not legalism. What I'm saying is that if we want someone to stop doing something, the best way is to love him and help him to learn a new way of acting.

Of course, there are emergencies when a person should be

106

told to stop right away. If someone has a bad relationship (adultery, homosexuality, promiscuity), there is a glaring need to call this person to repentance while offering the forgiveness and healing power of Jesus. If there are situations of public scandal, unforgiveness, slander, or divisiveness in the community, we are obliged to admonish those causing the evil. Usually such serious interventions are the pastor's business. However, all Catholics should remember that one of the spiritual works of mercy is "to admonish sinners." When we see our friend suffering from sin, we have an obligation in love to help him. Usually this would involve everyday things like shortchanging prayer time, community relationships, bad attitudes and neurotic patterns of behavior. Less frequent are the occasions when our friends are planning to do things which will clearly hurt their Christian life. This too is a moment for tough love, when we are willing to risk our friendship for the sake of calling people to remain faithful to God. Where plainly bad marriage plans or leaving community life are concerned, we might have to be strong to the point of harshness.

It is sad that people often fail to hold each other accountable in the big things (like marriage, community or prayer) and worry about little things (like punctuality, style of dress or talk). What we have to remember is that accountability is calling people to holiness, not to a particular kind of life-style. Because individuals need different things at different times, there can be no rulebook. We should pray for a genuine and affectionate love, discernment and wisdom so that our admonishment will be helpful and not harmful.

Admonishment is a powerful tool for building friendships and community. It is a tool we must use gingerly, however, always remembering that its power works to heal *or* to destroy. I've observed communities where it seemed that people spent more time rebuking than affirming each other in love. We have to keep in mind that we grow in our ability to receive and give correction in love. The more we feel secure in being loved, the more we can accept criticism. This means that we must allow people the freedom to make mistakes. The natural tendency here is to become paternalistic and to burden people with a standard of behavior that the Lord hasn't yet given them the power to live up to. Responsibility, patience and self-control are *fruits* of the Spirit, not of our will-power, and they take time to ripen.

In friendship this will happen as we learn to affirm, communicate honestly, disagree and challenge each other in the Lord. Keith Miller once said that "other people's faults shouldn't bother us until they bother them." Although this isn't always the case, there is a great truth here. Others' faults bother us because we see in them the image of our own weakness. They upset *my* schedule, ignore *my* needs, disagree with *my* ideas, distract *my* prayer. The danger of correction is that we want people to be holy so that we will have an easier life. Criticism born out of frustration and impatience is not admonishing one another in the Lord. It may be a good let-your-hair-down argument (and there's a place for that in friendship and community), but don't give it a sacred label; that would only grieve the Spirit. It's like the time a woman came up to John Wesley and proceeded to criticize everyone in her church and then called this the gift of discernment. Wesley replied, "Madam, I think the Lord would have you bury your talent."

St. Francis de Sales has a few hints on admonishing which helped me a lot. The first is *always to assume that the person has the best possible intention.* This applies to giving correction as well as receiving it. Since we can never be sure of a person's motivation, we can choose to look on his actions as well-meant. This has helped me to stop thinking of people's misdeeds as malicious and to see them as mistakes made through ignorance or weakness. Of course that's not always the truth, but the only way I can know if a person is willfully malicious is if he confesses it or the Lord reveals it to me (and that's very rare).

Another essential is a sense of humility as awareness of our goodness and sinfulness. If I am going to admonish someone, I should meditate on my own faults and confess them to the person so that he can feel that this comes from one sinner to another. Also, if I am being admonished, it helps to keep the extent of my sinfulness in mind. Like the time St. Francis de Sales was informed of particularly vicious criticism by someone and he responded, "If he really knew me, he'd have a lot more to say."

PRAYER

Christian friends pray with one another because they realize that their friendship can be maintained only through the power of God. If you don't want to pray together, perhaps God will still squeeze into the relationship. However, you probably won't grow as much unless you make your mutual dependence on God explicit. This means Christian friends recognize that there are some problems that our love and acceptance do not solve. We need a greater love in the times we cannot love. We need a deeper power to touch and heal the abyss of our sinfulness, and that is why we have to pray. Also, I find that prayer is simply more enjoyable with my friends, so that it becomes a necessary luxury.

Praying together does not guarantee that a relationship is automatically a Christian friendship. After all, it is perhaps easier to be unauthentic in prayer than in anything else. Prayer is not the proof that a relationship is holy but the way a relationship becomes holy. As in everything, the proof of holiness is love.

Now by praying together, I don't mean going to Mass or a prayer meeting together, although that is good and should be a part of a friendship. What I find most helpful is sharing conversational prayer with my friends, especially praying for my needs. Conversational prayer is usually more intimate, and it makes a lot of sense to me to use this kind of prayer with the people I'm most intimate with. That way I can share the deepest parts of my personality. I can thank God for the most personal victories and can feel that my friends share my thankfulness because they know my secret struggles. This means also that when I ask God for help, I can more easily trust that my friend knows my need and will sincerely pray for me. We can even see this borne out in the life of Jesus. In times of great joy or sorrow, Jesus, God and man, asks those closest to Him to come aside with Him. So we find Peter, James and John sharing with Jesus the glory of His transfiguration and the anguish of Gethsemane. And the agony of the garden reminds us all that

109

there are times when friendship fails and a man must meet life alone with his God.

Along with trust and intimacy of prayer with friends, there is furthermore the opportunity to open up to the power of the Spirit for the healing of our deepest problems. Prophecy, Scripture, inspired wisdom and insight are ways in which God can work with even two people in prayer. I find that prayer with friends lends itself to psychological healing and deliverance. This is because the warmth of being so knowingly loved and accepted makes us more receptive to God's salvific power. Also, my friends have a store of knowledge and experience which helps them to diagnose the roots of my problems. And because these are my friends, I sense that I'm still worthwhile even when confessing my weakness. The fact that they accept me and even enjoy my company helps me to avoid feeling that I'm just a problem, which can so easily happen with professional help.

Friendship also reveals our need for healing. The need shows up often through *conflict,* and conflict happens because friends try to be honest with each other and rarely settle for a superficial peace. I find I can fight with my friends and show them my anger and frustration. This helps me to get in touch with the wounded areas of my life. Also, my friends' frankness with me, while often producing some friction, lights up those things that need healing. I can't be phony with them. If I try a cover-up kind of prayer, like "Lord, help me to be sensitive to domestic values," a friend responds, "Yes, Lord, help Tony not to be so sloppy."

Of course this interplay of conflict and healing is much broader than what happens in prayer.

Just a few weeks ago a friend and I were talking about pre-marital sex. My friend repeatedly used words like "wholesome" and "decent." It just so happens that I can't stand those words, and I got very angry about what I thought was an attitude of moral superiority. As the disagreement progressed, I started to become aware that all of my earliest sexual experiences had been conditioned by what I felt were righteous, wholesome people making me feel perverted and unclean. I saw that all my life I had really disliked straight people because of this. The argument evolved into prayer for forgiveness and healing, and the defensiveness, guilt, and hurt left me to a large degree. Now, after the Sacrament of Reconciliation and further prayer with people who have a healing ministry, I feel almost completely free from that problem.

Prayer must be a regular part of our friendships. While it's not necessary that we pray every time we get together, I would think that some kind of structured prayer would be helpful, at least in getting started. The amount of prayer together depends on individual needs: for some, once a week; others, once a month. Still others are responsible enough to go beyond structure and to pray together whenever they feel the need. For a while, our group of friends from college got together almost weekly. Then we started going through different phases of growth and living situations, so we would only pray together rarely when someone suggested it. After three years of that, we once again meet and pray together weekly. In addition to that, all of us pray together frequently with our girl friends or wives and also in our separate households. What we've seen happen is a profound growth and evolving sense of purpose. God can deal with us in a deeper way as our shared love gives His power an opening to transform our whole personality.

COMMITMENT

Christian community places many demands on our time, and because of this we need a sense of the priorities of different time commitments if we are to grow. This is simply to say that some things are more important than other things and therefore deserve a greater share of our life. Your marriage is more important than your friendship, so you should devote more time to building that relationship. Likewise, friendships are more significant than television. This is a matter of finding a rhythm in life that creates enough growing space for the relationships you feel the Lord wants for you.

We also need commitment in our friendships, because we can't always trust ourselves to want to share or pray together in a regular way. The reasons for this are our laziness, stupidity, and the general human fear of being known in an intimate way.

111

Commitment carries us through the rough times. It doesn't create a friendship, but it nurtures it. This is to say that you can't make a promise to fall in love, but once you have fallen in love you need a commitment to help that love to grow. (Even as I write this, I can think of a few people who were so out of touch with their feelings that the only way they could fall in love with someone was to commit themselves to being with that person until a romantic love happened.)

Since we usually enjoy being with our friends, this commitment isn't often the grit-your-teeth variety. However, there are spells when our attraction to each other breaks down, and then those closest to us can hurt us the most. It's at these times that agape love takes over. Our commitment to work through problems is based not so much on friendship as on our loving each other as brothers and sisters in Christ. When we don't want to be together, we stay together anyway because we believe that Jesus wants it. This can work out like no other ideal, because we believe that the power of the Spirit will aid us when our own ability fails.

I've seen this happen with my group of friends from college. Within a year after starting a community life, half of us were feeling alienated and generally worn-out. We discovered that we could hurt each other in ways that we had never dreamed of in college. We had intense feelings of bitterness and betrayal. And we came close to physical violence more than once. Some had to leave just to maintain some semblance of sanity. Gradually the Lord healed us separately through prayer and counselling. It took at least another year till we were all comfortable around each other again. And only in the last year have we begun to see each other regularly and to try to pray together.

All of this has given us tremendous hope and confidence that we can, with Jesus, overcome any obstacle or hurt in our relationship. It's like a broken bone which, once healed, is stronger than it was in the beginning. We encountered our deepest fears in each other and through a lot of pain and prayer eventually conquered them. When you suffer together, for each other and because of each other, you know at last that Jesus' power is real, your love is real, and you are real.

112

JESUS IS LORD

Christian friends have to understand that their security, power, and hope are in Jesus. If they don't, they will find out quickly enough, since their relationship will probably fall apart or get painfully neurotic. It is only when we are secure in Jesus that we can let other people be free to be themselves. Otherwise, in our insecurity, we'll try to possess our friend. If we can't experience or believe in God's love, we'll settle for second-best and subtly demand that *our* needs be met, *our* problems be solved, *our* hunger for love be filled. This, of course, kills any relationship, friendship or otherwise.

Thomas Merton says that whenever we love someone or something more than God, our need for love increases a hundredfold and our fulfillment approaches zero. Our friends, art, nature, he says, are all reflections of God's love, beauty and truth. "They are like sunlight mirrored in clear water but if we try to drink the image, we only shatter the reflection."

Trying to find a savior in a friend kills the very joy and freedom of friendship. Fortunately, most people realize that they are not God and therefore cannot meet such demands. This frees them from the terrible burden of having to fulfill all of their friend's needs. Only Jesus can do that. There are times when we must say, "I can't help you; only the Lord can do that." Then we can direct each other to the Lord.

That Jesus is Lord of a relationship means that you explicitly agree that the only way it will completely work is through the power of the Spirit. Perhaps this entails talking to the Lord more than to any one person. It also includes a willingness to end or continue the relationship, depending on what the Lord wants. This leaves each person free to become the person God wants him to be. We are willing to let go if that is what God wants. We realize that we are not essential for that person's salvation. Christian friendship dies to itself in order to live in the "freedom of the sons of God." As Paul Claudel said, "It is not two people looking at each other, but two people looking together in the same direction and that direction is Jesus."

113

PLAYFULNESS

Everyone knows that play is for children — the children of God. We have an understanding in our community that people who pray together, play together. Unfortunately, our American mania for productivity clouds the fact that play and celebration are authentic and necessary expressions of what it means to be human. For Christians, play and laughter are a normal response to the Good News. We are set free from the burdens of sin, law, and having to struggle by ourselves. For many of us this means that we are free to play, to relax and be loved by God and friends. (Of course, there's still the bad news of evil, suffering and oppression; and our response to these is serious work and love.)

Play is done for its own sake. Play is wasting time, just as prayer is wasting time. Prayer is most truly prayer when we are there simply to be with God — for no other reason or function except to be with God. Play is wasting time with people (especially friends) simply because we realize it's good to have fun together. In both cases we can "let our hair down," be ourselves and laugh at ourselves. In both prayer and play we can be completely unself-conscious: our attention is focused on someone outside ourselves.

A sociologist, Peter Berger, says that play is one of the "signs of the transcendent" (cf. *Rumor of Angels)* in which we can experience a little of what eternity is like. We lose track of time in prayer and play; hours seem like minutes. "Time flies when you're having fun." This smacks of the Kingdom of Heaven where eternity is an instant because we are caught up totally in God's love. Similarly, the mark of the kingdom of hell is self-conscious boredom, where each moment becomes an eternity in the burden of isolation and fear. And there might be a special purgatory where the joy and laughter of the angels gently pries from us the last barriers of pride and self-importance so that we can fully enjoy God's love.

All of this is just to say that it is OK for Christians to play and have fun. It is natural for most friends to play a lot together. Games, laughter, parties, joking and even mock competition are the signs of friendship. However, there are some

Christians who would destroy all this for the sake of the serious mission of the Church. And the mission *is* serious; but we must always remember that we are not essential to that mission. Our efforts are not indispensable. The Lord is God. We need to take *Him* seriously, not ourselves. So it's good that Christian friends waste time on each other, enjoy each other. This, too, is a powerful witness, for often laughter can pierce the darkness more than our "important" words. This was brought home most clearly a few months ago when someone brought to dinner a few of his friends who found Pentecostals distasteful. We didn't know this and just welcomed them into our laughter and joking. We just shared our life together. The result was that these people perceived what God had done in our lives, and it probably changed a few of their ideas about Pentecostal Catholics. And we discovered two beautiful people to enjoy and share our joy with. This kind of thing often happens in our community. People come to a picnic, party or hoedown and are touched by the way we have fun together. Very often these are the people who would never come to a prayer meeting. Often, in this drab age, men need to see and hear our joy before they hear the Good News that gave it birth.

Another word for play is "re-creation." And this is what friends should do — help God re-create each other into being all they can be. In Isaiah Yahweh says that we were "designed for beauty." Christian friends should call forth that beauty in each other. Adrian von Kaam calls this "seductivity." All seductions use beauty to help us be vulnerable to love. In the same way friends seduce each other to grow and be vulnerable to God's love. Sharing our beauty and truth softens our hard hearts. Great music, books and ideas open us up to the loveliness and truth which is God. Very often this means helping others see their own attractiveness. We can imagine what our friends can become even more clearly than they can. We perceive the potential greatness in our friend, and we say to him, "You can be this." Where there are only seeds, we see full-grown flowers and say, "This is what you really are." Similarly, God encourages us to become what He already sees us to be — the full stature of Christ (Eph. 4:13). "Finally, my brothers, your

115

thoughts should be wholly directed to all that is true, all that deserves respect, all that is honest, pure, admirable, decent, virtuous, or worthy of praise" (Philippians 4:8).

Like all seductions, this must be done with tact, humor and grace. It can never be mechanical, or it becomes a bitter joke. In a sense it is a subtle play where we pretend to be new creations in Christ. And slowly, as we tell each other who we really are, we cease pretending — only to discover that we've become what we always dreamed we could be. "If anyone is in Christ, he is a new creation" (II Cor. 5:17).

DANGERS

On the whole, it would seem that particular friendships have been discouraged by spiritual writers. They are invitations to concupiscence, an offense to humility and charity. They breed divisiveness and are generally seen as something very dangerous. All these evils are quite possible. Friendships could be especially dangerous for the cloistered celibates for whom most of the warnings were written.

There is no doubt at all that spiritual friendship is a powerful and dangerous thing. Consequently, it should be approached with the greatest respect. But then, so is marriage powerful and dangerous; so is a career and even Christian community. All of these things can hurt you and harm your union with God. The key is learning how to handle these things in the Lord. You set up a few safeguards, watch out for danger signals, respect always the power of what you're involved in, and, above all, pray intensely. In many ways it's like using nuclear power for peaceful purposes. There's great danger but even greater benefit.

What I want to do at this point is to list some common dangers and helpful ways to cope with them.

SPIRITUAL ADULTERY

I think it was Ralph Martin who coined the term "spiritual adultery" to describe a relationship which psychologically and spiritually violates a marriage commitment. This danger arises when only one of the marriage partners becomes involved in a more intense Christian life. There is now something vitally important which is seemingly impossible to share with wife or husband. "How can you communicate the joys of prayer, the struggles of community, the humor of certain leaders when your spouse might not even believe in God?" After a few enthusiastic attempts to bridge the gap, which usually alienate the couple even more, religion is relegated to the list of unmentionable taboos. Perhaps the other spouse feels threatened by this new involvement which seems to be pulling his or her mate further and further away. There might be subtle efforts to have the more explicitly Christian partner drop these new activities. In this cycle of isolation, one or both of the partners might seek compassion and understanding from someone else. This is a good thing to do — up to a point. However, what can happen is that one or both end up regularly sharing parts of their life with someone other than their spouse. Since marriage is supposed to be the blending of your whole life with another, this kind of exclusive intimacy is in a sense adultery. It can also very easily lead to physical adultery.

Most people do not perceive this psychological closeness as a danger to their marriage. They enter into it sincerely trying to fill their need for personal sharing and counselling. *But the problem is that it is more intimate than the marriage relationship.* This does not mean that you have to share with your spouse everything you would confess to a priest. It does say that the marriage relationship should be overall the deepest, most intimate relationship you have. If it isn't, the problem isn't with the outside relationship. The problem is in the marriage. The solution demands a greater effort to communicate from the marriage partners. There's a need for sensitivity and tact, especially if one of the spouses is not explicitly Christian. This means that the Christian experience should be shared as revealing who I am, not as an attempt to convert the other. If this is done without a judgmental attitude on either part, there's a good chance that alienation won't creep in.

In our community, we've seen tremendous success in this area and also tremendous failures. The key to the whole problem is the quality of the communication between the spouses. There are people in our community whose spouses are either non-Christian or involved in a different style of Christian commitment. Because the community members have respected their spouses' religious beliefs (and vice-versa) and have consistently shared what's going on in a non-threatening way, the spouses feel that they are somehow a part of the community. A big factor in this was their meeting the community in a non-religious situation. Whether it was going out for a drink or moving a house full of furniture, they started to have some kind of relationship with community. The Christian community itself can help to avoid problems if its members approach the family with an attitude of service, not preachiness. It's pretty hard to feel suspicious about people who come to lend a hand when you're in need.

All I'm saying is that if there is a good marriage where each person communicates and is flexible, there shouldn't be any crisis. The problems usually arise in the marriage where there might not have been any real communication for decades. With some couples, any outside relationship except a passing acquaintanceship is more intimate than the marriage relationship. In such cases, I think it would be rather inhuman to condemn a person to only the superficial kind of relationship in his marriage. Where one of the partners is unwilling to communicate, there is a tremendous need for compassion and sound spiritual direction. A small group of people (preferably of the same sex) could profitably share with this person. Hopefully, as he or she grows in the Lord and learns how to handle relationships, a friendship with someone of the opposite sex may develop in time. This might seem to be putting it a bit too cautiously, but the dangers here are so great that it's wise to go slowly. We've seen disasters when married people plunge into such friendships recklessly. Also, we've witnessed how healing it can be for a person in this situation to have a deep friendship with someone of the opposite sex. Both the cautions and the hope would apply to people in a separated, divorced or celibate state of life.

As to how to reach the non-communicative partner, the first and second chapters of I Peter offer a Christian strategy to transform marriages and all society. The key here is loving service by husband or wife (or slave). It is very much like Gandhi's non-violent revolution. By continuing to love in seemingly impossible situations, we witness the power of God. Spouses and all society can see the difference God makes because we are joyful in a situation which would drive anyone else insane. This is obviously not a law we obey by our own efforts. This witness of slow martyrdom is only possible through much prayer and the power of the Spirit.

SUPERFICIALITY

Then there is the problem of slipping into a rut in the relationship. A friendship stagnates when friends need to stick to "safe" subjects of conversation, to avoid risks and unknown territory. This situation comes about when we stop sharing our gut-level feelings. What we do then is to use our common interest as a kind of mask to hide what's really on our mind. "We can still enjoy our intellectual conversations, jokes or sports without having to reveal all of those uncomfortable things, can't we?" Well, we probably can. Sometimes the chance to do low-risk things together gives us a breathing spell and helps to heal us. More often, if it lasts too long, it hinders our chance to grow.

I notice the rut when I fear that I won't be understood. It takes too much time to communicate what's really going on in me. I even convince myself that the best way to love my friend is not to burden him with these problems. As a result, I put on a kind of forced joviality, talk about interesting subjects and reminisce — all without really encountering my friend. The resulting isolation is far worse than any problem I could have burdened him with. Now he might feel there's something wrong in the relationship. Perhaps he did something to make me angry and I'm afraid to tell him. What I have to do at that point is to take the risk to believe that my friend cares about me almost as much as I care about him. If he were in this situation, I would want him to share with me. So, trusting in that love, I should open up to him. However, I almost never take this step until my friend prods me out of my phoniness.

119

One way of avoiding ruts is to talk about what your defense mechanisms are. Gradually, after being together for a while, you get to sense when your friend needs to be challenged or cuddled. Great sensitivity is called for here, since we both crave and detest another person really knowing us. (There will be more about this in Chapter 3 of *Freedom in Christ).* The whole solution to superficiality is a matter of trusting one another enough to let yourself be known.

We need to learn how to believe that somebody loves us. This takes time and perseverance. We make many mistakes. Friendship will periodically go stale. This is not the end of the friendship; it is usually just a plateau that needs a little more effort to traverse.

Very often we jump out of communication ruts by means of conflict. Isolation can so encrust us that only something explosive will break us out of it. Non-communication causes friction the way an infection causes pain. A toothache warns us that something is wrong. If we ignore the pain or try to suppress the conflict, there's a good chance that someone might be harmed. Conflict can be very creative or very destructive, depending on how you handle it. (Read *The Intimate Enemy: How to Fight Fair in Love and Marriage* by Dr. George R. Bach and Peter Wyden. This book lays out guidelines and safeguards for controlling the power of conflict.)

Being aware of our tendency to superficiality and learning communication techniques are just the beginnings of open friendships. *The basic way for a Christian to learn how to be a sensitive, loving friend is building a long-term relationship with Jesus in prayer.* In prayer we learn how to encounter a person, to be present to Him, to focus our attention on Him and to dialogue. Prayer teaches us how to wait, to listen, to take the good days and the bad. Prayer integrates us, joins our mind and emotions in love, teaches us commitment. In prayer we encounter the mystery of God and learn that our mental boxes are much too small ever to contain Him. So we gain the humility that lets us be surprised as God reveals more and more of who He is. At the same time we are learning how to encounter and enjoy the mystery of our friends. Prayer is the

120

ultimate communications workshop, because we are experiencing the Person who is most a Person, who touches us in the depths of our own personality.

This is not a one-way street, nor does prayer have to come before friendship. Our openness and love with our friends prepare us for the Friend. Friendship helps us to pray, and prayer helps us to be friends. I've experienced it both ways. As far as it could go, friendship helped me to receive love when I became aware of Him. However, there were definite limits to my ability to relate to people, and it was this weakness that needed the power of prayer. For one thing, I feared boredom. I could never believe that any person could be interesting enough to hold my attention day in and day out. Of course this changed, as Jesus taught me how to be open to the mystery of His person. He schooled me through dry spells or deserts in prayer. Here I learned that you can't force a person to reveal himself; you have to be patient and let the person be free. This was excruciating. Most of my life I had considered myself to be very open, and I expected and often demanded that others be just as frank as I was. I had a compulsion for emotional honesty which dictated that other people should be honest whenever I wanted to be honest. Well, I soon learned that Jesus, as well as my friends, didn't respond to my emotional choreography. As God had planned it, this happened precisely at a moment in a deep relationship with a girl when I needed to wait and be patient. I discovered how to enjoy the mystery of another person. This mystery is so deep that we can always discover more about who that person is. If you are immersed in mystery (divine and human) you are protected from superficiality and boredom.

EXCLUSIVENESS AND CLIQUES

> *People who bore one another*
> *should meet seldom;*
> *People who interest one another, often.*

(The Four Loves, p.116)

This quip by C. S. Lewis might not seem to be very Christian at first glance. It does, however, exhibit a great deal of realism and compassion, both of which are very Christian attitudes. It also points out why friendship is always selective and why this selectivity can turn into exclusiveness. Friendship is based on common interest. What interests one person, however, bores another. If you are not caught up in the friendship's common interest, you automatically feel like an outsider. The reason for that is that you *are* an outsider. The same thing happens when you listen to two people talk about a mutual acquaintance whom you don't know — you are bored and very much left out. Now, it's very rude and unloving to ignore a companion this way. If the two friends had any sensitivity at all, they would have included the third person in their conversation by talking about something all of them have in common. That many people are blind to this kind of sensitivity is the reason why exclusiveness is the plague of friendship in Christian community.

In friendship and marriage there is an authentic need for people to have time together to share. It's just like finding time for personal prayer. You try to do it in a way that doesn't alienate people. For example, if someone comes to you in great need, you don't tell him to stop back in an hour because you have to pray. However, if you are merely engaged in light conversation, you shouldn't feel hesitant to say that this is your usual hour for prayer. Hopefully, you would trust your fellow Christian enough to ask that of him. In the same way, we are called to be ready to give up the time we spend with our friends for the sake of our partner in marriage, or to trust our Christian community enough to ask them to leave us alone to share together. There are no set guidelines as to when and how we should do this. It is a prudential decision based on each one's discernment of the situation. We will make mistakes and possibly hurt feelings. This is to be expected since mistakes are a normal way to find God's will through a process of elimination. And when we can't quite follow Jesus, at least we can stumble after Him.

It is a normal part of life that friends and lovers find time to be alone to share. Common sense tells us, however, that this should be at times and places which do not give the impression that others are left out. Large parties, prayer meetings or liturgies are not occasions for intimate sharing. These are community experiences where we should try to relate to the people we ordinarily wouldn't encounter during the week. Especially in public worship, Christians should be overly sensitive to welcome strangers and practice hospitality. This does not mean that every time you go to dinner or a movie with a friend it constitutes an open invitation to everyone. Sometimes it should. At other times you can excuse yourself because you need time to talk. We would hope that God wants loving marriages and friendships as well as a loving community.

There is a great need for balance here. On the one hand, we must build relationships, and on the other we have Jesus' teaching:

He said to the one who had invited him: "Whenever you give a lunch or dinner, do not invite your friends or brothers or relatives or wealthy neighbors. They might invite you in return, and thus repay you. No, when you have a reception, invite beggars and the crippled, the lame and the blind. You should be pleased that they cannot repay you, for you will be repaid in the resurrection of the just."

(Luke 14:12-14)

To fully understand this, we have to look at Jesus' actions as well as His words. Amazingly enough, He said this to His host, one of the leading pharisees. It seemed to be directed as a correction for an obvious fault. He seems to be communicating what kind of attitude we should have, since He Himself did not literally practice these words. After all, Jesus did not invite the pharisees to the last supper.

Real exclusiveness is when we do not welcome people at any time. A clique accepts only the right people. An open friendship rejoices whenever it finds someone else with the same interests.

A clique does things like:
—staying together at public meetings and parties;
—refusing to ever let anyone else join in their activities;
—considering their friendship to be a mark of superiority;
—attempting to exert a kind of political pull in community life.

Friendships can easily turn into cliques unless the friends make a conscious effort to maintain other community relationships and to welcome new friends. The same kind of exclusiveness can happen in a marriage. Or in a God-and-me clique. Again, the attitude of openness and readiness to welcome strangers in any form is the dividing line between particular relationships and cliques.

Lastly, there is a sociological principle at work. Robert Nesbit in *Quest for Community* points out that *large groups do not like smaller groups.* Small groups threaten unity and uniformity. Whenever possible, the large group (United States, Church, Prayer Community) tries to negate the power of the smaller groups (States' rights, religious orders, friendships). The reason for this is that the larger group knows that revolutions are always started by small, special-interest groups. The support and sense of identity that friendship gives is a force that can be turned against the larger group. It robs the large group of its power to form its people, because the people no longer identify with the large group but find more meaning in their special-interest group where their personal needs are satisfied, Also individuals not involved with the special-interest groups are often alienated from and resentful of the small community; and so they join with the large community to repress the "clique." Added to all this is a fundamental non-communication where people ask:

Why do they always stick together?

What do they do when they're together?

Why can't we join in?

Why can't they be like the rest of us?

This kind of dynamic is at the root of all kinds of prejudice and persecution. Ethnic groups, religions, scientists, religious orders and friendships have all been victims of this at one time or another. And that a community is Christian is no guarantee that it will not in some way suppress friendship for the sake of uniformity.

So, then, the things to keep in mind are:

1. Friends and married people need time together in the same way that all of us need time for personal prayer.

2. This time together should be structured in a way that doesn't give other people the feeling of being left out.
3. This needs to be balanced by the greater command to love all men, especially the needy.
4. There are sociological tendencies of:
   a. cliquishness—friendship will exclude all other people.
   b. the large group suppressing friendship for the sake of uniformity.
   c. non-communication causing individuals to help the large group suppress friendship groups.

SEXUALITY

First of all, our sexuality is not a problem. It is a gift of God. It is a gift which is usually trying to express itself. We are thoroughly sexual beings, and the only danger is when our sexuality interferes with our primary commitments in life. I understand the Gospel as calling us to express our sexuality within the limitations of the particular states of life that we have chosen as single, married or celibate people.

The danger of sexuality in Christian friendship is that, when you really love someone intimately, you have a very great desire to express that love sexually. This is normal, and it is probably a sign of health that you would have a sexual attraction for a friend of the opposite sex whom you love. Love and sex are supposed to go together. The only question is: what do you do about this normal, healthy, God-given attraction? Christians have tried a number of solutions. They are:

1. Avoiding all possibility of sexual attraction.
2. Ignoring and suppressing your sexuality.
3. Casting your morals to the wind and indulging yourself to the full.
4. Recognizing the attraction and trying to deal with it.
5. Asking for God's power and healing.

Avoidance and suppression

This is the old routine of: "If I don't look at it, it will go away." Somehow the idea got around that if a Christian even talked about sex, it was almost a sin. Another variation is:

125

"Heathens do those things; it can't happen here: we're Christians." However, Christian behavior through the centuries has amply demonstrated our humanity in this respect. It's comforting to know we're still human beings, but it's also sad to remember some of our glaring failures. For example, in the early Church where the Spirit was really alive and you could tell who the real Christians were, St. Paul writes: "It is actually reported that there is lewd conduct among you of a kind not even found among the pagans — a man living with his father's wife" (I Cor. 5:1).

Things like this happened in every age, from Abelard and Heloise to Aimee Semple McPherson, and they happen even now. Keith Miller relates how he was shocked out of his naivete by a minister and his secretary (both married) who confessed to having committed adultery during a retreat. They never thought it could happen to them.

If we choose to have intimate friendships, we must be aware that these kinds of things can happen to us. It's like driving a road at night. If you are aware that there's a dangerous curve ahead, you will slow down and be more careful. Sometimes Christians think that just because they pray together they will never be sexually attracted to their friends. Often it's just the reverse — the more you share with someone, the more likely it is that you'll feel sexually attracted. Martin Hollenweger cites an interesting example of this in his book *Pentecostalism: the Charismatic Movement in the Churches.* It seems that in America in the 1940's, young men would wait outside the Pentecostal prayer meetings hoping to pick up one of the girls, because after praying they seemed to be an easy make.

A few years ago, after I gave a talk where I mentioned this whole subject, a woman came up and said that this could never happen to her relationship. She and her friend had a "purely spiritual relationship" and they were "beyond all that." She had never felt any sexual attraction to him at all. Since she was a very holy woman I believed her. About a month later I ran into her again, and she said simply: "You were right — thank God nothing disastrous happened."

So, we can't ignore the dangers in friendships. Yet we

shouldn't be afraid either, since Jesus gave us His Spirit to overcome our weakness.

Indulge yourself!

This is obviously ridiculous for a Christian. However, some people have bent over backwards trying to rationalize self-indulgence with the Gospel. An example from Knox's *Enthusiasm* is a small sect called the Brethren of the Free Spirit. They had an interesting interpretation of St. Paul's teaching that to have sexual relations with a prostitute would be to join the Body of Christ to the body of a prostitute (I Cor. 6:15). Their extremely logical conclusion was something like this: "It would be sinful if a woman were to have intercourse with her husband who was not a believer, since he is not a part of the Body. However, it would not be sinful if a woman were to have intercourse with a brother who was not her husband, since he is a part of the Body of Christ." The humor here dims somewhat when we realize that a recently founded sect is using the same logic to justify their immorality.

Recognize our sexuality and try to deal with it

This approach usually works better than the previous ones. It involves regarding sexual attraction as a normal part of intimacy. This means that it isn't traumatic when you realize that you are sexually attracted to someone. It also entails taking a hard look at the everyday facts of our sexuality.

First of all, whenever your relationship with Jesus is on the rocks, you are bound to feel insecure and crave affection. For me this seems to be the time when I'm most vulnerable to a sexual encounter. Physical affection becomes the way that I feel affirmed and loved. Also, it is natural to want to comfort in a physical way someone else who is depressed or having psychological or marital problems. For example, if a person feels that his spouse does not understand him, he is fairly open to fall in love with the first person who listens to him. At this point he would probably fall in love with a telephone pole if it had an ear.

Whenever we are in a period of psychological and physical

stress and weakness, we are very vulnerable to sexual affirmation. I'm sure that this is because God intended sexual love to be a great comfort and relaxation. This applies to times of great fatigue, when we're overextended or just slightly drunk. If you realize that this is normal, you can be especially attentive at these critical moments.

A very big part of coping with our sexuality is not taking ourselves too seriously. We must be able to laugh at our sexual drives to realize how much they are conditioned by our physical and psychological states. I happen to be a person who falls in love very easily and very emotionally. Since I know this, falling in love ceases to be a great trauma that compels me to change my basic commitments. I've learned to chuckle at this very fickle part of my personality. Most of all, I realize that these grand passions won't last more than a month; so I view them with great skepticism.

This is especially true when a married or celibate person forms a friendship with someone of the opposite sex. For example, two married couples in our community had been meeting and praying together regularly for over three years. At one point or another all of them became aware that they liked the other's spouse far more than their own. They talked and prayed and laughed about it and continued to be faithful to their marriages. One of the husbands said that he realized that if he were married to the other woman, he would probably have the same problems with her that he had with his wife now.

On the whole, you could probably say that the importance of sexual sins has been overemphasized. Again, much of this is due to the fact that most of the theology and spiritual writing has been done by celibates for whom sexual sins were tremendously destructive. What they understood was the *power of sexual relationships to change or destroy our lives.* Sexual passion can help transform us into whole and loving people, or it can make someone forsake everything else of importance and plunge his life into ruin. *However, the possibility of destruction lies not in our passion but in our response to passion.*

The question, then, is not how do we avoid or diminish passion, but what do we do about it? A perfect example of this was a psychologist's response to a patient who had a compulsion to feel sexually desirable and was trying to seduce him. "Don't you want to make love to me?" She asked. "Yes, I want to make love to you," he said, "but I don't think that I will."

When you fall in love, you *want* to forget about your marriage or celibacy; but you don't have to do it. Even if you have had some kind of illicit sexual relationship; don't act on it. Don't think that this means you have to leave home, family or ministry for the sake of your beloved. You failed, but don't compound the failure by building your life around a mistake. If you make love to someone, you don't have to follow it up with a trip to the marriage bureau. If you commit adultery, you don't have to get a divorce. Even if it's a homosexual experience, it doesn't mean that you must change your basic life commitments. Confess your sin. Seek spiritual direction and pray for the healing of your relationships. Don't let your sinfulness control your life; let Jesus.

Ask for God's power and healing

Fortunately, we don't have to depend completely on our own common sense and will-power to direct our sexuality. We can never lose hope, because "we have the mind of Christ" (I Cor. 2:16) "whose power *now* at work in us can do immeasurably more than we ask or imagine" (Eph. 3:20). Practically this means: (1) We are given the charism and power to live chastely in our state in life (married, celibate, single). (2) God will heal us of the physical and pyschological weaknesses which might lead us into sexual irresponsibility.

(1) The demands of chastity in marriage, the single state and celibacy are unrealistic if we must rely solely on our own will-power. That route often leads to neurotic suppression, legalism, or failure and guilt. Our choosing to be chaste should open us up to the Spirit who gives us the power to be chaste. That this is widely misunderstood is witnessed by a great number of divorces, lost vocations and forced marriages. People find themselves with difficulties in chastity and rarely ask God to give them the power to help them out of it. They lose hope and perspective and forget that:

No test has been sent you that does not come to all men. Besides, God keeps his promise. He will not let you be tested beyond your strength. Along with the test he will give you a way out of it so that you may be able to endure it.

(I Cor. 10:13)

The first step is believing that God would want to help you be sexually responsible. This was very difficult for me. I hated the whole idea of chastity for a long time. It had too many old-fashioned connotations. After a few failures and many frustrations, I realized that most of this area of my life was being directed by my fear and insecurity instead of Jesus. It was only within the last two years that I finally asked God for the power to live a chaste life. After much prayer and struggling, I still do not feel that I myself have the power to control this area of my life. Without Jesus the most I can do is try to keep the law. With Jesus I can actually want to be chaste and go beyond the letter of the law. In either case I can't be self-righteous (I've failed too much for that). I try to remember Paul's advice about being tested: "For all these reasons, let anyone who thinks he is standing upright watch out lest he fall!" (I Cor. 10:12)

(2) Many times we need to be healed of psychological problems so that we can be sexually responsible. Sometimes we have such crippling and deep-rooted problems that our responsibility is diminished and our will-power can't help us out. This is when we need healing. Things like homosexuality, promiscuity, chronic masturbation or other aberrations are not freely chosen sexual preferences but symptoms of deep-seated fears in our psyche.

As regards friendship and sexuality, the problem areas are probably limited to our compulsions for sexual attention and the problem of homosexuality.

Many times the intensity of our sexual need is based in neurosis and a poor self-image. We crave sexual attention to achieve security. We may feel that we can believe that our friend loves us only if he makes love to us. What is needed here is the healing of the memories which produced that compulsion. Most

130

often they concern our relationships with our parents.

As to homosexuality, I only have two things to say. First of all, this is a real problem in Christian community. It has been overlooked and indirectly encouraged by our preoccupation with the danger of heterosexual relationships. By frowning on male-female friendships (especially for celibates), we direct people to intimacy with people of the same sex. Simply in terms of time and circumstance, it is a lot easier to have a homosexual affair in Christian community than it is to have a heterosexual affair.

Secondly, there is in Jesus healing for this problem, which gives people the hope of having a healthy sexual life and not just the burden of struggling to avoid sin. An example of what God can do here happened a while ago in a counseling situation. This man feared any kind of friendship because every time he made a friend (male or female) he ended up in bed with him or her. He was afraid he could never have a normal life because of the power of this compulsion. He had had some homosexual experiences as a young man, with the result that he was so insecure in his masculinity that he attempted to seduce every woman friend he had. His guilt also led to a chronic problem of masturbation. After confession we prayed for the healing of these old memories, and he was completely relieved of the guilt. Now there is every indication that he can lead a normal life, and with the help of his community he is learning a new way of relating to his friends. So, whatever our problem, God will give us a way to live within our state of life with freedom and responsibility.

DEALING WITH DANGER

Although I've already mentioned a number of ways of coping with the dangers of friendship, I want to summarize a few more that we have found especially helpful.

PRIORITIES IN COMMITMENTS

The basic principle we've used in relationships is simply to "seek first the Kingdom and everything else will follow." This means that by making sure that your relationship with Jesus is your No. 1 priority, the impact of most problems will be greatly

131

diminished. Threats still exist, but you can handle them peacefully, with confidence in God's power. Most of the dangers we have talked about become destructive because Jesus is no longer Lord of our life. When we lose this radical openness to Jesus, we start to become insecure. When we're insecure, we become possessive and make saviors out of our spouses, our friends and even our community. This is when all the "fruits of the flesh" (Gal. 5:19-21) start to appear in our life. I can't stress strongly enough that *the only way Christian friendship works is to make our primary commitments more important than the friendship.* First of all, is our relationship with the Lord loving the Lord with our whole heart, mind and strength? This does not necessarily mean that we *feel* more love for God than for our spouse or friend. It means that we depend on God more than we depend on people. It means that our security is in His love and not in our relationships. In a pinch we will choose God's will over the desires or demands of our spouse or friend. Utlimately, it means that we are willing to terminate a relationship if it is destroying our relationship with God.

In terms of marriage and friendship, our friendship can never be more intense than our marriage relationship. If you have a weak marriage, than a strong friendship will threaten the security of the marriage. You can see this every day. Imagine two married couples at a party. The first couple is very insecure about each other's love. The husband starts talking to an attractive divorcee, and immediately the wife runs over to protect her husband from this threat. The second couple has a very secure and trusting relationship. When this husband talks to another woman, perhaps an ex-girl friend, his wife doesn't react. Because she is confident of her husband's love, she can let him form other relationships without being threatened. She can even admit that this other woman might fulfill some need in her husband that she can't fulfill (i.e., work association). Because of the strength of their marriage relationship, they are both free to form other friendship relationships. *For Christians, the depth and security of their primary relationships with Jesus and their marriage partner is the depth to which they can form friends outside those relationships.* Schematically, it would look like this:

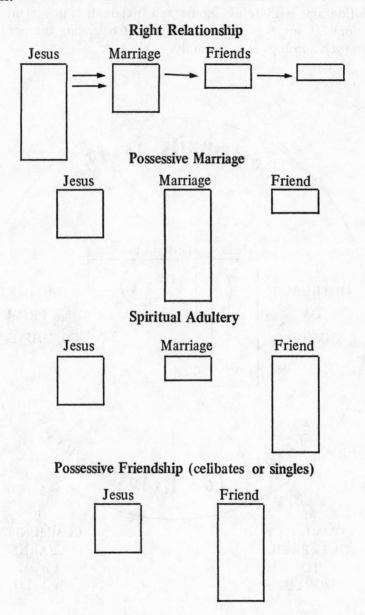

Right Relationship

Jesus   Marriage   Friends

Possessive Marriage

Jesus   Marriage   Friend

Spiritual Adultery

Jesus   Marriage   Friend

Possessive Friendship (celibates or singles)

Jesus   Friend

I haven't mentioned community as a particular relationship because I see community as the whole context and arena for our relationships with Jesus, spouse and friends. It is important here to look at some guidelines in terms of balancing the needs of these relationships in community.

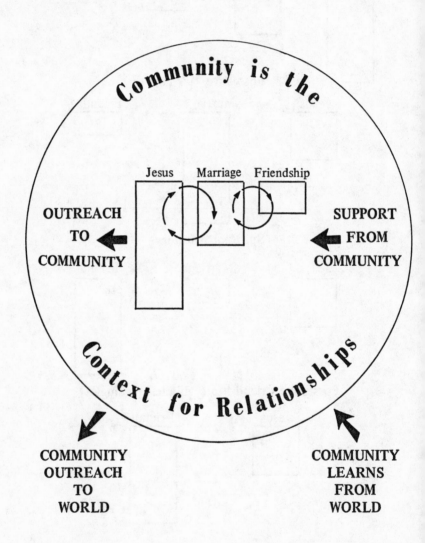

Relationships are always a two-way street; we both give and receive; i.e., our relationship with Jesus helps us to have a good marriage and our marriage builds our relationship with Jesus. In the same way, a good marriage allows us to form deep friendships, and our friendships enrich our marriage. The depth and security of all these intimate relationships help us reach out to the community, and in turn the community supports our primary relationships. And a strong, loving community reaches out to love the world, and because of its basic security can learn from the world. So, to list some guidelines:

1. Jesus is primary relationship.
2. Marriage subordinate to relationship with Lord.
3. Marriage (sacrament) *co-ordinated with relationship to* community (sacraments of initiation).
4. Celibacy (can be sacrament) subordinated to God-relationship (sacraments of Baptism, Eucharist and Confirmation). Celibacy = service to community.
5. Friendship (non-sacramental) subordinate to God-relationship, marriage and community.
6. World outreach subordinate to community relationship.

SPIRITUAL DIRECTION

Most of us have little perspective on the quality of our deep personal relationships. This is the reason why psychiatrists are usually not very adept at analyzing their own families. This is also an excellent reason why Christians need direction for their friendships and their whole spiritual life. We need someone who can pierce through our own self-deceptions to guide us into the truth. We also need someone who is wise enough to know the different phases of Christian life and how to respond to them. And this person needs to be open to the power of God so that we will be healed of the problems that talking doesn't cure.

For spiritual direction to work, we need the faith to accept our director as an important channel through which God shows us His will. We also have to be absolutely honest. Spiritual direction most often occurs with a priest or minister, with confession a normal part of the relationship. If we can't find a ministerial director whom we feel comfortable with, we can talk things over with a wise and holy person whose discernment we trust. In any case, it is critical to share what's going on in our relationships so that we can get a balanced perspective. I have a spiritual director whom I see from time to time, but I find that most of the sharing on what's happening in relationships takes place with my different friends. Most importantly, we discuss our relationships with the opposite sex. Here we share not only the common joys and trials but also try to help each other find God's will in these relationships. Sometimes this entails blunt and challenging questions. These can hurt, but it helps all of us to face what we're about as Christian friends. A few times, I have been strongly advised by friends to break off certain relationships. Once I didn't and wish I had. The other times I did and I'm still grateful for the advice.

These are a few of the things in which spiritual direction can help us. We need common sense when our emotions have overwhelmed our reason. We need to be encouraged to hang in there, and sometimes we need to be told to break it off. Without a sounding board, the resulting isolation might lead us (and our friends) into a very unpleasant darkness.

CALL TO RESPONSIBILITY

Friendships happen; we can't structure this happening into our life. However, we can do some things to help us be more open to beginning new friendships. First of all, we need to pray and trust that God will fulfill our needs. This means that for Christians, friendship isn't just a matter of blind choice. Neither is it simply the result of our good taste, background, intelligence or culture. These are all the raw materials that God uses to bring people together. As C. S. Lewis says, when Christians discover friendship, "they know that the Master of ceremonies has been at work" changing chance into providence. I have seen in my own life that God has a delicacy for timing and circumstance that leads us to the right people at the right time. And he who has numbered the hairs on our head is sure to be lovingly careful with so large a concern as our need for friendships.

This means that we should relax, be ourselves and   not

force this issue. Aside from being the Christian response to the Father's love, this is also the easiest way to develop friendship. If we simply go out to people, initiate conversation and try to find out what they are like, then friendships will most probably happen. As we learn to play and share who we are in a more effortless manner, we may be surprised at the people we find as friends. People who on first impression seem so bland one day, open up to be a storehouse of joy and love.

Perhaps I have made too much of friendship as common interest and have neglected the friendship of diversity. Here we are delightfully awed and occasionally enraged by a person who seems to be our polar opposite. These might be the friends from whom we learn the most. In our life we shall probably find many friends, different kinds for the different seasons of our lives. All we need to do is develop our capacity for surprise and mystery.

Especially in the beginning of our Christian life, there is a time to break off bad relationships. Most of the time we only need to let them atrophy. If the friends are explicitly non-Christian, this might often happen simply because we are trying to follow the Lord. What happens is that the values and perspectives that created the friendship are no longer shared. You don't see eye-to-eye on things anymore. Old projects have lost their interest. The result is that you no longer share a common vision on what life is about. It could happen that an old friend might even try to inhibit your Christian commitment. At this point the relationship must be broken. As a matter of fact, any time a friendship runs counter to your primary commitments in life, the friendship should be aborted. This is hard but necessary. Everything we have said about the supportive power of friendship can work to lead us away from our Christian commitments. Compromise is very dangerous here, for there is a siren's call to friendship which coaxes us to "stay the same, don't change, be one of us." To resist this lure requires a very difficult and very concrete choice to say no.

The necessity for this kind of responsibility was brought out on a recent retreat. One of the exercises was to chart our spiritual life over the last 5 years. Almost every person there found that his lowest times were when he was involved in a bad relationship. The point here is that not all relationships should be saved. Sometimes we are not open to solutions; other times our friends are hard-hearted and the Lord can't get in. It might be the wisest thing in some instances (possessiveness, sexual problems) simply to give up and run. At times, humility demands that we say that something is too big for us. This is not necessarily cowardice or lack of faith. After all, the Apostles didn't wait to be martyred in every town they went to, sometimes they sneaked out. Martyrdom pursues us; we don't have to seek it in destructive relationships. Only when we hear the Lord ask us, *"Quo vadis?"* "Where are you going?" do we, like Peter, return to the martyrdom we have avoided for so many years.

We are also called to change old relationships to Christ-centered friendships. This usually takes a long time. Our friend or relative has to see a substantial change in our lives before he can relate to our Christianity as real. If we have tact, honor and a sense of self-criticism, we are usually able to share our Christianity with old friends. This does not necessarily mean they will convert in the same way we have, but Jesus can be part of the relationship. However, when old friends make a Christian commitment, we need to renovate our friendship with prayer and witnessing. All in all, we need to take seriously the ways in which God wants to work in our friendship and to expend the effort to make this real in our lives.

DIFFERENT WAYS OF RELATING
TO EACH OTHER IN COMMUNITY

Three years ago, during a retreat for Oblate seminarians, one of the men shared what has become for me the best description of the foundation of community life. He said that he had been trying to be one with his community for years but had always failed. During the retreat he came to a realization: "I can't share my intellectual, cultural or social interests with each one of you. What I can share is my relationship with Jesus; and if we all do that, then Jesus will make us one." Christian community is basically about loving each other as the Lord loves us. Our oneness is not so much through our intelligence, programs or techniques. We are one because all of us share Jesus and experience His Spirit. Community is both the gift of God and the work of man, but without the gift we have nothing.

This might be a solution to the age-old human dilemma — "What do we talk about?" How do I relate to those people who do not share my special interests? What do you say to someone you don't like? How are you one with him? This was a crucial test for me, since before I fell in love with God, I felt that 90% of the people I met were rushing bores. Two things have happened to change this: (1) God changed my heart so that I felt interested in the mystery of these people, and (2) I discovered that I could share my relationship with Jesus with everyone in the community. This is the basic thing we can talk about; this is our common union. I'm not crazy about so and so's passion for antiques, but we share all the experience of being on the same adventure together. He is not wild about my fairy tales, but he and I can talk about what's going on in the community. Because we do not choose the members of our community, there are bound to be people with whom we have little in common. In trying to relate to everyone on the wrong levels, we might end up simply gossiping and politicking. It can happen. Sharing our relationship with Jesus at least gives us a very important way to relate to every member of the community.

Over and beyond this, the particular way that people choose to relate to one another is a matter of individual discernment and life situation. This applies to styles of community. Perhaps the Trappists would rightly think all our insistence on communication techniques to be unnecessary. The diversity of spiritualities arises from our situation, needs, service, and discernment as to what perspective we should take in the Christian community.

We might need, and be led by God, into forming community through developing household living situations with a clearly structured system of authority. There would be less of a need for friendship here, since most of our time is spent relating to the members of our household, and loving support is felt in the leadership. Or we could have a community which is structured into small sharing groups, and again the need and opportunity for friendship diminished. This could be a structure of very close service teams where people share the faith together. Or it could be in neighborhood groups or in terms of the support and intimacy of the nuclear family. In any of these situations, the style depends on the community's own understanding of how Christians should relate to one another.

WHY FRIENDSHIPS?

Our community understanding of the need for Christian friendships is hopefully a response to the Lord as we read the "signs of the times." Bishop Fulton Sheen has said that Christendom is dying and leaving a new kind of Christianity to emerge risen. In the world today there exists no longer the stable pattern of tradition, custom and law which has led to the formation of stable local communities. The "Sacred Canopy" which protected and made possible the kind of geographic faith communities of the middle ages is no longer real for people. Instead we have a highly mobile, rapidly changing society where long-term commitments are the exception rather than the norm. Christians have to resist this super-fluid tendency in society, but we are still to an extent at the mercy of the economic and political realities of our times. And whole cultures do not change overnight. In the megalopolis it is difficult to choose who your neighbors will be, so we need a different response to meet this situation. Sometimes the Lord will create the circumstances in which geographic community is possible. However, on the whole I think it would be safe to say that most of the people involved in Christian renewal can't, won't or shouldn't form this special kind of local community.

Most of these people are already members of a local community structure in their parishes and congregations. And for Catholics it looks like the parish structure isn't going to change in the immediate future. Christian friendship provides a way that people can develop faith-relationships in the midst of this present situation.

We see friendship as a more organic and flexible way for the large majority of Christians today to find growth in relationships. There are problems here. But at least they are interesting problems that challenge us to grow. As Lewis said, "Only the man who is asleep or dead has no problems. Mistakes are simply the sign that we are awake and not asleep, that we are alive and not dead." The question of Christianity is not "How do we avoid problems?" but "How do we find solutions?"

BIBLIOGRAPHY

RECOMMENDED READING:

St. Francis de Sales, *Introduction to the Devout Life,* Image Books, Garden City, New York, 1950, 315pp.
   *A spiritual guide for everyday laymen, this 17th century classic has an excellent section on friendships (*Part 3, 19-22*). Some may have problems with the style.*

Lepp, Ignace, *The Psychology of Loving,* Helicon Press, Baltimore, 1963, 223pp.
   This is an in-depth, clinical study of love, sexuality, marriage and friendship by a renowned priest-psychiatrist. Although a bit too Freudian, it is excellent in describing the complexities of love relationships.

Saint Exupery, Antoine de, *The Little Prince,* Harcourt, Brace & World, Inc., New York, N.Y., 1943, 113pp.
   A delightful, mysteriously beautiful fantasy on love, friendship, death and other essentials of life.

SUPPLEMENTARY READING:

Greeley, Andrew M., *A Future to Hope in,* Doubleday, Garden City, New York, 1969, 286pp.

Worshipping Community

Here Fr. Greeley examines the basic religious problems of modern society and outlines some positive Christian solutions. Especially relevant to this chapter are his chapters on "Sex to Love with" and "A World to Play in," where he gives a rich and often poetic analysis of friendship and celebration.

Hendricks, Howard G., with Ted Miller, *Say It with Love,* Victor Books, Wheaton, Ill., 1972, 143pp.

A very practical, corny yet funny book on the nitty-gritty of loving and witnessing. Loaded with anecdotes, it still manages convincingly to criticize the lack of Christian love.